SILVER
The Five Road Ends

A memoir of a 1940s childhood in a North Staffs mining village

GRAHAM BEBBINGTON

Foreword by John Abberley

CHURNET VALLEY BOOKS
1 King Street, Leek, Staffordshire. ST13 5NW 01538 399033
www.leekbooks.co.uk

ISBN 9781904546795

ALSO BY THE SAME AUTHOR

The Loggerheads Project (Newcastle Borough Council)
Pit Boy to Prime Minister (University of Keele)
A Brief Life (Isle of Wight County Press)
Trentham at War (Churnet Valley)
Ship Without Water (Churnet Valley)
The Fledglings (Churnet Valley)
Trentham Reflections (Churnet Valley)

Acknowledgements

First and foremost, I would like to thank my friend the late John Abberley for writing the foreword to the book. John was a valued source of encouragement and inspiration over the years for which I will be forever grateful.

In addition to those quoted in the text or source notes, I am most appreciative of the assistance of the following:- Councillor George Cairns, Richard A. Durrant, John H. Emery, George Valco, Frank D'Arcy, Bill & Dorothy Hughes, Professor Ray Johnson, and the Editor and Staff of *The Sentinel*.

I acknowledge use of photographs from *Life on the Dale* by Barry Williams, published by Churnet Valley in 1999.

Gratitude is also expressed to Mrs D.M.A. Randall, Head of Archives, Staffs. County Council; Mrs D. Copp, Curator, Newcastle Borough Museum; the librarians and staff of Newcastle, Trentham, Hanley & Holmcroft Libraries.

Finally, my wife Lynne Margaret has, as usual, shared in all the pleasures and pain of research and assisted with everything from IT consultancy to being my soundboard throughout.

Every endeavour has been made to trace source material. If inadvertently any copyright has been infringed, the author offers his apology and will correct omissions in any subsequent edition.

Cover photo by Claude Hadgett (1982).

CONTENTS

FOREWORD

Silverdale was a good place in which to grow up, says Graham Bebbington. Few people will disagree with him after reading this loving portrait of a mining community which has now passed into history.

But was life 'on the dale' really as good as all that 60-odd years ago? You'll have to decide for yourself. We all remember the best times from the past, although Graham has done rather more than that in a book which runs to 32,000 words.

Rarely can so much have been remembered in detail about life in an industrial village, whether it's the predominant colliery, the male voice choirs (Kathleen Ferrier sang with them at Silverdale), the very individual bus services, district nurses, the ice cream parlour, local characters like Communist Fanny Deakin, or the way they coped with rationing and growing their own food.

The Five Road Ends of the title was Graham's playground, the centre of the universe to Silverdale children. Coming from the same generation, I can recognise such a place, though in my case this sacred patch was in Hanley Park.

Graham hits the nail on the head when he talks about the privilege, no less, of growing up at a time when kids could roam freely without worries about traffic or predatory strangers.

It was indeed rich compensation for the privations of a working-class childhood in the 1940s, when food was basic, children played games like marbles or hopscotch and those who owned a bike or a football were kings of the castle.

What stands out for me about this author is the care he takes to get things right. This is the reward for painstaking research, which has been his trademark over the years I have been watching his impressive progress.

He is a writer who takes his time, whatever subject he tackles, and there have been many. This is his eighth book since he left his job as a Council officer at Newcastle. He has put the freedom which comes with retirement to good use.

Graham Bebbington's latest book is the sort many people would like to write about their own childhood. But few have the dedication or the skill to complete the task. In that sense The Five Road Ends is an object lesson to us all.

John Abberley 2010

INTRODUCTION

Not so long ago, I read a letter in a national newspaper from a child. She wrote of being taught at school the meaning of the word ‘freedom’ ie ‘living in a free country, freedom of speech, free democracy etc’. However, having learnt from her parents what a happy childhood they’d had - ‘able to wander freely everywhere without being harmed, disappearing from their parents’ view for hours on end to make the most of the long summer days, being able to play in the streets and so on,’ the child observed that she couldn’t do any of the things that her parents spoke of. There were restrictions to everything, or there appeared to be! For example, she was unable to go out anywhere without being escorted for fear of paedophiles, neither could she play in the streets because of the traffic. So, she asked ‘where was the freedom?’

I couldn’t forget the letter, and it inspired me to record some of my own childhood memories. It emphasised to me how privileged I was to have been born in the period that I was, and the location of my birth. I cannot consign to oblivion the halcyon days of my youth on the dale - the sense of its strong community and so tightly knit, memories of the humour, colourful language and camaraderie of life amongst the miners and villagers. To me, Daleians are as genuine as the Staffordshire oatcake.

GB

‘able to wander freely everywhere without being harmed, disappearing from their parents’ view for hours on end’

Drawing courtesy of Adam Ridgway from *A Potteries Lad* by Bill Ridgway

Vicarage Bank (now Pepper Street) - the entrance to Silverdale from Keele - in the 1940s. One of the pit slag-heaps is seen to the left. *(Brian Nixon).*

One
Waiting for the Fuhrer!

I was barely twelve months old when Prime Minister Neville Chamberlain broadcast to the nation at 11.15am on 3rd September 1939 that 'this country is at war with Germany.' Other than having heard copies of the historical recording, I naturally do not recall the event!

War clouds had loomed over the country for some months and the British people had studied the news from Europe as one might survey the skies in an attempt to predict the weather. Journalists had frequently used the term 'war clouds gathering' but it all seemed so far away. However, this air was abruptly shattered by the Premier's broadcast announcement of the declaration of war.

Throughout that summer the preparations for war had, in fact, began to intrude inexorably into everyday life. Ration books, identity cards and public information leaflets containing such advice as *The protection of your house against air raids; If the invader comes* and *Masking your windows* were among the depressing official publications dropping through letterboxes. Buildings were suddenly adapted for alternative use, such as first aid posts etc., and in the streets air raid shelters and sandbags became familiar sights.

Plans were enacted to evacuate children from areas thought to be at risk of bombing and, despite censorship, the local press reported that some of the earliest arrivals in Staffordshire were from the Ramsgate, Broadstairs and Margate areas.[1] Some evacuees arrived at Silverdale, the O'Dell family from Leyton in London being placed with my long-time friend Alan Scott and his mother in High Street. Alan informed me that Mrs O'Dell and her daughter Maureen came initially, but were later joined by the grandmother. To this day, Alan can't imagine how they all lived in the two up, two down terraced property!

At that time, Alan's late father, Sgt Tom Scott was serving with the Royal Artillery in Italy and one of his Battery received a letter informing him that his family had been evacuated to Silverdale and were living with a family named Scott in High Street, Silverdale. I'm certain that there is a mathematician somewhere who could calculate the likelihood of this happening!

Certain Government departments were also evacuated, and twelve Regional Defence Commissioners were appointed with special powers to govern their areas in the event of invasion. Furthermore, if the need arose, the Cabinet Office was to be relocated at Hindlop Hall, Worcester with Parliament itself at Stratford-on-Avon. Other plans included the transfer of the BBC's main centre to a country house in Worcester and the storage of some of the National Gallery treasures in a cave at a disused quarry in North Wales. Similarly, local museums made plans to transfer precious items to alternative 'secret' depositories. Stoke-on-Trent City Museum arranged to remove certain artefacts to a property at Gravenhunger on the Staffordshire-Cheshire border.[2]

In consultation with the Treasury, the Bank of England had also made plans to relocate various operations, and part of its Dividend & Loans offices were established at Barlaston Hall, Stoke-on-Trent. The Bankers' Clearing House, the nerve centre through which cheques passed to and from every part of the country, was also evacuated to nearby Trentham Gardens and renamed the Central Clearing House. This major operation took place on 26th August 1939 and involved the transportation of one thousand employees and equipment by rail and road.[3]

Other friendly 'invaders' included the Fleet Air Arm whose training establishment HMS Daedalus II 'sailed' in with five hundred apprentices and ship's company, establishing themselves at Clayton Hall. They arrived in May 1940, a necessary move due to wartime, but the rural tranquillity of the sleepy village of Clayton was never again restored.[4] In fact, during this period, thousands of foreign troops also arrived in North Staffordshire which had a profound influence on the life of the area.

In the months preceding the outbreak of war, some 38 million gas masks were distributed to the populace, including Mickey Mouse faced ones for young children and complete respirator suits for babies. It was an offence not to carry a gas mask at all times, but as the war progressed and a gas attack did not materialise, the only occasions that the public tended to wear them was in practice drills or mock attacks. Had I been fortunate to have been given a Mickey Mouse model, I'm certain that my parents would have had no difficulty in persuading me to wear it! On the village, the political campaigner Fanny Deakin helped to distribute gas masks and instructed mothers in the use of children's masks. Fanny was also an Air Raid Precautions Warden, the Head Warden for Silverdale being Ralph Sutton of Abbey Street.[5]

Another important aspect of Civil Defence was 'the blackout.' In order to make it as difficult as possible for enemy aircraft crews to sight their targets, windows had to be covered at night so that no chink of light escaped. Streetlamps were fitted with a special screen which dimmed their lights, and vehicle headlamps were similarly treated to project downwards. In addition, names were removed from railway stations, public buildings, post offices etc and signposts and milestones uprooted in an attempt to baffle any likely invader. Buses at the beginning of the war stopped carrying destination indicators and at Silverdale, the sign at the County Primary (or Board) School was boarded over for the duration. Despite these well intended gestures, addresses could still be found in public telephone boxes and some manhole covers were embossed with local authority names. Also, some shops continued selling postcards showing and naming local scenes!

In preparation for war, Parliament passed the Emergency Powers (Defence) Bill on 24th August 1939. This resulted in over 500 new laws being introduced onto the statute book, placing restrictions on almost every aspect of life. Amongst other things, these included imposition of curfews, whether rare birds should be de-protected to enable eggs to be consumed in times of food shortage, control of the country's finances and the internment of any 'whose detention appears to the Secretary of State to be expedient in the interests of public safety or the Defence of the Realm.'

A Conscription Bill had been introduced earlier in May 1939 and soon afterwards all young males under the age of 21 were registered, ready to be called up for military service whenever required. As the war progressed the age of conscription widened to include men between the ages of 18-50, but also single women between 20-30. Most conscripted men were destined to serve in the army and by June 1941, approximately 2.25 million were in uniform. Our family was no different and relations were drafted into the services and armament factories. However, my father and certain other relatives were exempt conscription on account of being employed in the coal industry. This came within the purview of an Essential Work Order or 'reserved' occupation. Others such as farmers and train drivers were also exempt military service. Even women at home looking after children, the sick or the elderly were expected to contribute to the war effort by undertaking such tasks as assembling small machine parts. In some areas, children's schooling could be interrupted, and they had to contribute in a variety of ways such as assisting with harvesting or collecting materials for recycling.

Whilst new factories were being built, or old ones being re-equipped to reinforce the country's war machine, organisations such as the Observer Corps and Local Defence Volunteers (LDV - later the Home Guard in July 1940) were coming into their own. The former were trained in identifying enemy aircraft in addition to being alert for signs of invasion. The Corps was affiliated with the military and acted as extra eyes and ears, relaying information to Fighter Command from their local HQ bunker off High Lane, Alsagers Bank. News of the approach of any enemy aircraft was then conveyed to Silverdale via sirens on the roofs of the Roxy cinema and the children's nursery in Vale Pleasant.

Patrolling and enforcing the blackout was a major task of the ARP Wardens who, in Staffordshire, came under the command of Lt. Colonel W.J. Kent.[6] They wielded a curious power, for contravening the blackout could land you in court with a hefty fine to pay. Dressed in navy battledress and a tin helmet, and equipped with gas mask and torch, they were the butt of much wartime humour. Nevertheless, these personnel also had to deal with the immediate aftermath of a bomb falling in their area, informing central control, organising ambulances, fire and rescue services etc. In addition, they were expected to administer first aid and to ensure that people remained calm at any incident. The ARP were also responsible for public air raid shelters in their area, the local HQ on the village being the Infants' School in Mill Street which had been requisitioned under emergency powers.

Staff of the First Aid Post which was based in the requisitioned Infants' School, Mill Street, Silverdale during World War II. Dr. Percy Johnson is in the second row, fourth from left. *(Newcastle Borough Museum).*

Breaches of the blackout were strictly enforced under the Defence Regulations and reports in the press indicate a number of cases where fines were imposed by the Borough Magistrates. One in particular related to a property in Wolstanton Road, Chesterton where a Mr L. O'Neil was fined the sum of £5 for displaying a light during blackout hours. The Magistrates noted that he had been previously convicted for a similar lighting offence.[7]

The local Member of Parliament for Newcastle-under-Lyme was Colonel J. C. Wedgwood. Being a member of the LDV, on one occasion he entered the House of Commons having omitted to remove his armband. Later that day when he arose to ask a question, other Members in the Chamber 'loudly cheered' on seeing the item of uniform.[8]

One year on and by September 1940, the war had affected everyone through absence or loss of loved ones, changing patterns of life, shortages and rationing of food, clothing and household items, and the constant fear of invasion. This fear was finally realised when bombing raids began on British towns and cities. The country was no longer an island fortress. The stretch of water which for centuries had been our first line of defence could now be breached. Once hostilities actually began, the nearby market town of Newcastle-under-Lyme suffered isolated bombing raids by the Luftwaffe, the first being on 26th June 1940 at Gower Street where a 4 year old evacuee was killed two days after arrival. The irony is that he came to the area to escape the horrific bombing in the south. But bombs and rockets do not differentiate between persons, and children were neither spared death nor injury.[9] Similar incidents

John Street, Chesterton following bombing by the Luftwaffe December 1940. *(Newcastle Borough Museum).*

occurred in the town later in the year at Keele Road and then at John Street, Chesterton, resulting in extensive damage and numerous casualties including evacuees, this time from London. The raids were reported in the press but due to censorship were only identified as having taken place at 'a Midland town.' Similarly, whilst the press reported sympathy having been expressed at local Council meetings, locations were not identified.[10]

Silverdale appears to have escaped lightly in relation to bombings by the Luftwaffe with the exception of a bizarre incident which occurred on the night of 5th May 1941 resulting in the death of a 20 year old woman. For some reason, the home of Eunice Stubbs at 17 Newcastle Street was the target for a lone incendiary bomb. Intentionally or otherwise, the unexploded device hit the roof and fell into the room below, passing through the bed in which Eunice was lying, and then buried itself in the kitchen table on the floor below. Local barber Jack Deakin, in his role as an ARP Warden, was soon on the scene with Dr Percy Johnson. According to information subsequently passed by Jack to his son Michael, the girl was still alive on their arrival but severely injured, and she was pronounced dead at the North Staffordshire Royal Infirmary.[11] Her tragic death appears to have been the only recorded fatality resulting from hostilities which occurred on the village; her name is inscribed on the war memorial at St. Luke's Parish Church.

Times being what they were, one could perhaps be forgiven for thinking that my parents could have chosen a more ideal time to plan a family - bless them.

Notes

1) Staffordshire Advertiser 13th July 1940
2) Sentinel 28th August 1939
3) See Trentham at War (Churnet Valley Books) by this author
4) See Ship without Water (Churnet Valley Books) by this author
5) Newcastle Borough Council (NBC) - Air Raids Precautions Committee 30th Nov.1938
6) Sentinel 25th May 1940
7) Staffordshire Advertiser 6th July 1940
8) Sentinel 25th May 1940
9) NBC records: 'Casualties due to War Operations.' The deceased was John Stobart from Romford.
10) Staffordshire Advertiser 21st December 1940
11) NBC records (as in 9 above). Although four other people were registered at the property, namely Alice Stubbs, Edward Stubbs, George Arthur Stubbs and George Dodd, there were no other casualties, according to official records.

Bomb damage at the Corona Pop Works, Sandford Street, Chesterton December 1940. *(Newcastle Borough Museum).*

Bomb damaged properties in John Street, Chesterton. December 1940. *(Newcastle Borough Museum).*

TODAY'S HAPPENINGS:

Getting Ready For Any Emergencies

POSITION IN NEWCASTLE AND DISTRICT GENERALLY

"Standing by for any eventuality," has been the position of Newcastle's A.R.P. services since last night.

During the morning, while broadcast bulletins were announcing the bombing of Warsaw and seven other Polish cities and towns, an emergency meeting of the Newcastle A.R.P. Committee was being held to complete preparations for eventualities in the borough.

During the night a skeleton staff manned the Report Centre at the Municipal Hall—nerve centre of Newcastle's scheme.

Throughout to-day, work has been proceeding at preparing the various posts and depots, including sand-bagging them. While first-aid posts, wardens' posts and other depots were not manned, the personnel has received "Stand by" instructions and full arrangements could be in operation in a few minutes.

In North Staffordshire generally to-day, the hospitals have been in process of being put on an emergency basis, work proceeding according to plans previously arranged.

The first North Staffordshire platoon of the National Defence Companies, recruited only yesterday, paraded for duty this morning.

It is hoped that Newcastle will furnish at least one platoon to this force, open to ex-Servicemen between the ages of 45 and 55, and acting as a Territorial Army Reserve.

The 104 Group of Companies, which embrace all those recruited in an area extending from Wolverhampton to Birkenhead, is commanded by a well-known Newcastle resident—Lieutenant-Colonel G. A. Wade M.C.

LONDON BANK CLERKS IN TRENTHAM

Many London banks, insurance companies and business houses have transferred their headquarters to the country.

During last week-end streams of lorries carried essential books and documents out of London while recalled staffs were helping to pile sandbags against office windows.

Large numbers of people in the Potteries have taken in London bank clerks as lodgers.

Among the London bank clerks transferred to the country are 1,100—400 of whom are women—who have been sent to Trentham, where their new headquarters are the ballroom and restaurant.

It was announced yesterday: "They are to stay for at least six months whether war breaks out or not."

Veterans Flock To The Colours

Headline of the Newcastle Times. 1st September 1939.

"SPITFIRE CORNER"

"On to the second thousand," is on the lips of every Spitfire enthusiast in the borough, and the Deputy Mayor (Councillor George A. Heywood), in his capacity as chairman of Newcastle's Spitfire Fund, has set an admirable lead with the slogan "He gives twice who gives quickly."

Only eight days to reach the £1,000 mark is good going, but efforts are not to be slackened, for speed is on obvious necessity.

By the courtesy of the Newcastle Corporation, the fund has been granted the use of a shop on the Island Site, to be known as "Spitfire Corner," where contributions will be gladly received

The garden party held at Red Heath, Silverdale, realised £101 and a contribution of £13 has been received through Mr. L. G. Fetzer, Secretary of Newcastle Chamber of Trade, from the Globe Cafe, Ltd., High-street.

To-morrow and Monday the "Mile of Shillings" effort will take place.

At the committee's request, Wolstanton Traders' Association are organising local efforts on behalf of the fund, to embrace Wolstanton, May Bank and Porthill districts.

Fund-raising event at Red Heath House. *Newcastle Times* 6th September 1940.

Red Heath House, Silverdale then residence of Councillor J. H. Ramsbotham and the venue for many fund-raising events for the war effort. *(Alan Scott).*

Evacuated children arriving at Newcastle railway station, September 1939. *(The Sentinel).*

Winston Churchill inspecting Home Guard at the House of Commons. *(Author's collection).*

Clifford Corbin on civil defence 'duty' outside an Anderson shelter. Humour prevails despite the war - he holds a toy gun and sits on a tricycle. *(Islwyn Corbin).*

Evacuee Maureen O'Dell with Alan Scott. *(Alan Scott)*

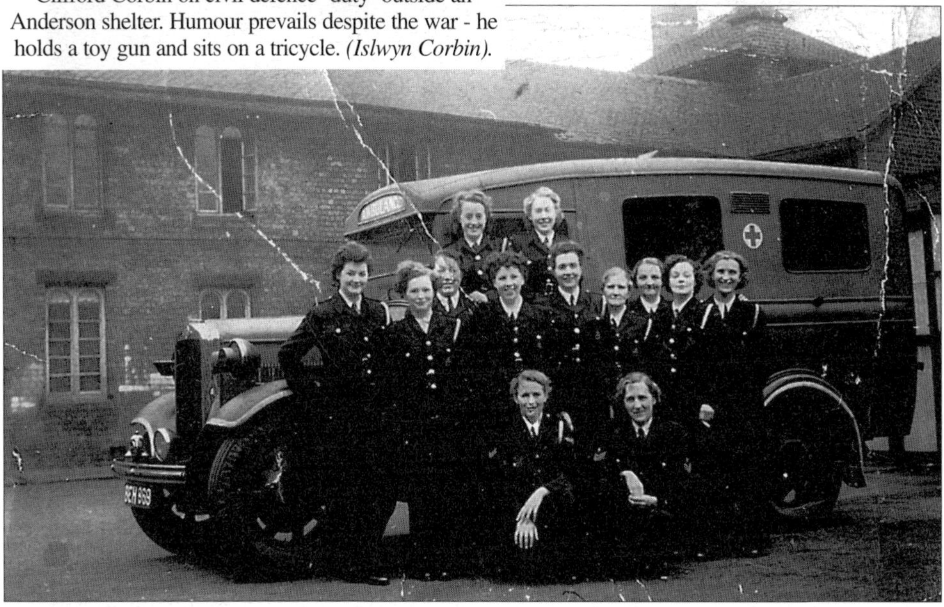

Newcastle-under-Lyme Civil Defence Ambulance Unit at the Barracks, Newcastle. *(George Shaw).*

Paul Robeson (left) with co-star Edward Rigby in a scene from Ealing Studios film *'The Proud Valley.' (National Film Archive).*

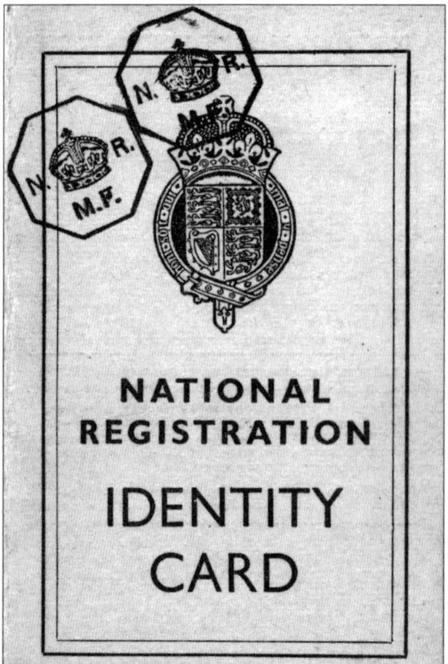

Author's collection.

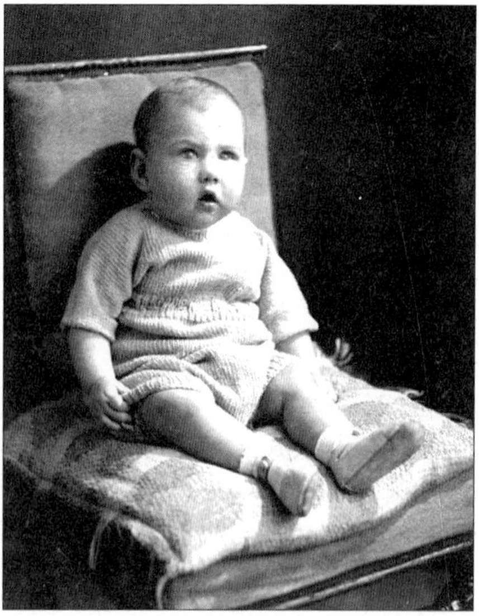

'War - what war?' The author contemplates the situation!

Two
Born on the Dale

I was born at an early age in the mining village of Silverdale in North Staffordshire - on 23rd September 1938 to be precise. With the pleasant soft green of the hills rising to Keele on the southern side, and that of Gorsty Bank on the north, the village nestled in a valley approximately two miles from the market town of Newcastle-under-Lyme. Affectionately known as 'The Dale', it was a community built on coal - 'a child of the industrial age' to quote a former teacher.

Yet, in my youth, despite having some industrial scars, Silverdale was far from being an unpleasant place in which to live. The countryside was never far away and there were agreeable walks in thc vicinity, even within the shadow of the pit banks. The miners particularly took advantage of these walks, not only to take in the magnificent views, but also to inhale in to their lungs the fresh air carried in by the winds from the sea and across the Cheshire Plain. Walking through the Kents Lane colliery complex to join Footpath No.103, one could ascend Gorsty Bank through the fields, passing the slag heap often likened to an extinct volcano, and onto Blackbank Road where a stile afforded a magnificent panorama of the Apedale Valley and the Potteries conurbation beyond. This was used by some as a place for contemplation or meditation. It was up there that one could put problems into perspective by looking over the countryside. What had happened to you, or was likely to happen to you, was insignificant. It had all had worse troubles than you and survived. Spend a little time up there with the wind in your face, and you had no problems at all. Some simply referred to it as 'God's country.'

Climbing further up Blackbank Road to nearby Scot Hay or Alsagers Bank, the views were breathtaking. One could view the best kind of country from up there, the kind of landscape featured in the leading topographical and guide books. From the Newcastle side of Alsagers Bank, the hills between Leek and Buxton were visible to the north east and in the opposite direction, Titterstone Clee Hill in Shropshire. From Scot Hay and Alsagers Bank the land sloped gently towards Leycett, Betley and the plain of North Shropshire and South Cheshire. On a clear day looking to the south and south west, one could pick out such landmarks as Caer Caradoc, Long Mountain and Llanymynech Hill

The Parish Church of St. John, Keele rebuilt in 1868 at the expense of the Sneyd family. Keele remains a popular walk from Silverdale. *(Author's collection)*.

Whitmore with its 17th Century timber framed church and hall, the residence of the Cavenagh-Mainwaring family. *(Author's collection)*

At play with the Mullineux sisters - Janet at the rear with Evelyn Thomas and Christine, Cheryl in front with Alan Wilkinson & Keith Berry. *(Christine Ward).*

Playmates outside the Pop Works gates, left to right Keith Berry, Josie Bateman, Doreen Berry & the author, with Ronald Walker in front. (Norah Walker).

The former Eight Row cottages in High Street, Silverdale. To the left is the Vine Inn which survives today. The white building to the right is the former Roxy Cinema. *(Alan Scott).*

Chapel Street with Edwards' accumulator charging shop at the Five Road Ends, photographed by the late Harry Corfield just prior to demolition in the early 1950s. *(Hadgett Collection).*

Thomas Wilkinson, founder of the family shoe repairing business, pictured here outside the shop & family home in Church Street, Silverdale.
(Harold & Alan Wilkinson).

BELOW
The former Gothic Houses, Church Street, Silverdale (from *Life on the Dale* by Barry Williams).

An early postcard showing High Street, Silverdale at its junction with Sneyd Terrace.
(From *Life on the Dale* by Barry Williams).

The Sneyd Arms, High Street, Silverdale affectionately known on the dale as the 'Bush'.

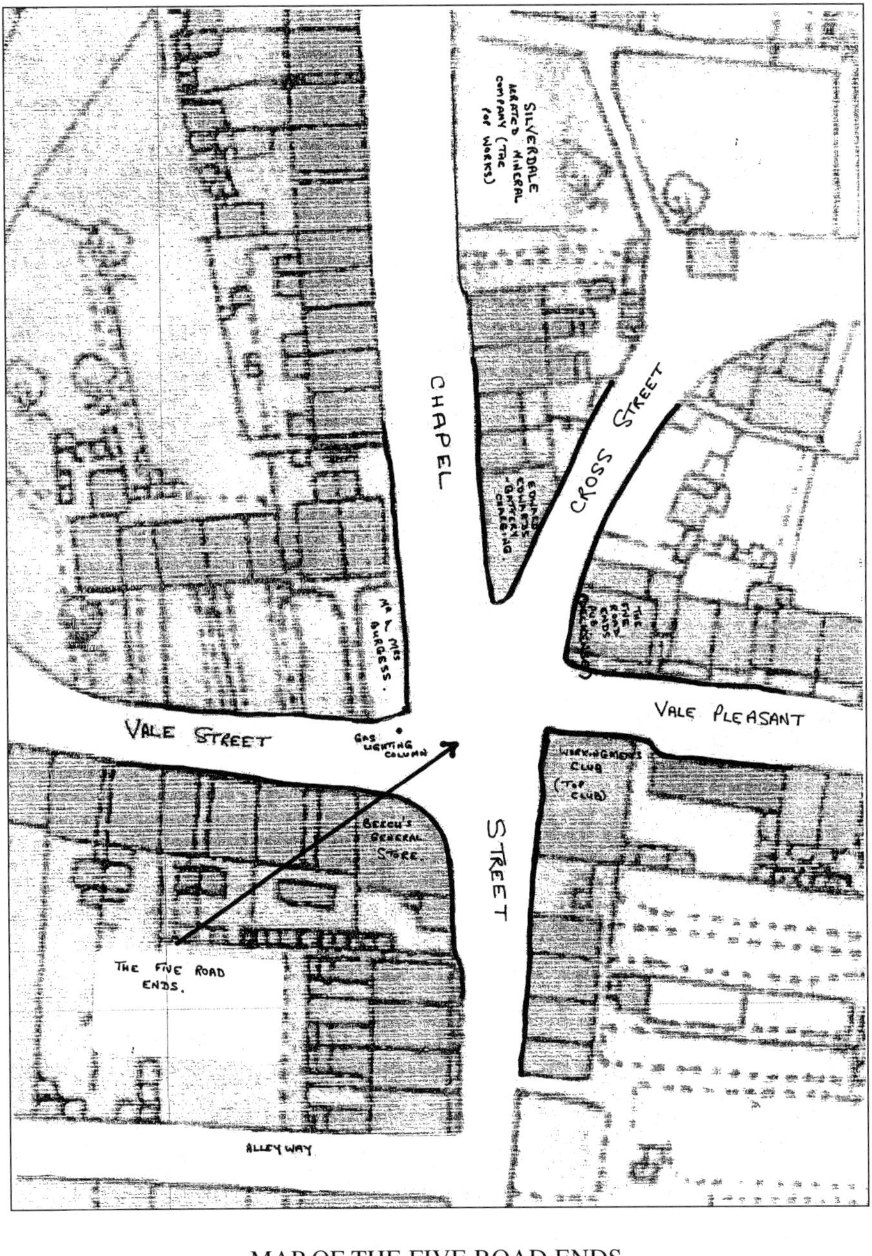

MAP OF THE FIVE ROAD ENDS.

overlooking the valley of the Vyrnwy.

Another much appreciated viewpoint was Spring Bank, a pleasant hilltop approximately 1.5 miles west of the village, reached via Hollywood Lane or Crackley Gates. Spring Bank stood alone from the general range of hills and on reaching the top, the Cheshire Plain spread out beneath one's feet like a magnificent carpet. I've heard villagers claim to have seen ships in the Mersey estuary from this point on occasion. Spring Bank was another place of peace and quietness where one could enjoy the air. The late Harold Brown in his classic book *Most Splendid of Men* wrote of how as a young miner he remarked to his father what a magnificent location Spring Bank would have been for a hospital for the miners and those suffering from dust diseases. Tough miners were known to have flung themselves onto their backs in the lush grass, gaze up at the blue sky and inhale the invigorating clean air. It was also known as a place where those in local choirs could rehearse their parts with little chance of disturbance.

One could also view the Cheshire Plain when walking in Keele. Moel Fammau, highest peak in the Clwydians could also be seen from there on a clear day. From Two Mile Lane views of Keele Hall, former residence of the powerful Sneyd family since the 16th Century, could be obtained. During my childhood it was occupied by American service personnel and remained so for the duration. For the more energetic, the attractive village of Whitmore, with its 17th Century timber-framed church and hall, could be reached via Three Mile Lane.

According to some, Silverdale had the air of a Welsh mining village. This was particularly so perhaps in the first half of the 20th Century when the village was not as large as it is today, not having experienced redevelopment of its central area. It is also worth noting that Silverdale was featured as a Welsh mining village in the Ealing Studio film 'The Proud Valley', a role it shared with Mardy in the Rhondda Valley. Starring the great Paul Robeson, production commenced in August 1939 at Mardy, but there was difficulty in finding a pit which would permit locational filming. The situation was resolved when the Shelton Coal, Iron & Steel Company gave permission for use of its Silverdale

OPPOSITE PAGE:
SILVERDALE ENTRIES FROM KELLY'S DIRECTORY OF STAFFORDSHIRE FOR 1940.

PRIVATE RESIDENTS.

Boydell Frank D. 175 High street
Cocks John, Silverdale house
Ellams Mrs. M. Sneyd villas, High st
Emery Ernest, Park fields
Johnson Miss G. A. 173 High street
Johnson Percy George M.B., Ch.B. The Bungalow, Mill street
Kirby Rev. Robert (Roman Catholic), The Presbytery, Downing street
Lowndes Frederick William, The Hawthorns, Park road
Morris John Sydney, Sneyd villas, High street
Moss Rev. Frank Anderson B.A. (curate), Westbrook, High street
Nicholson Victor Rylands, 177 High st
Ramsbottom John, Red Heath
Sheldon Rev. Harry Christie B.A. (vicar), Vicarage

COMMERCIAL.

Early closing day, Thursday.
Marked thus ° farm 150 acres or over.
Allman Herbert, pork **butcher,** 13 Church street
Amison Mary Jane (Mrs.), fried fish dlr. 105 Church st
Ashton **Wm. plumber, 83 Church st**
Bailey Harry W. beer **retlr.** 81 **Victoria st**
Bailey Jn. Fredk. seedsman, 7 Newcastle st
Barker Arth.P. stationer,24 Church st
Barratt Samuel Harold, dentist, 106 **Church street**
Barratt Thomas Edward, dentist, 118 Church street
Barratt Wm. cycle **dlr. 104 Newcastle st. T N 56**
Basford Wm. butcher, 81 High st
Beech Caleb, grocer, 1 Vale st
Bennett Nellie (Mrs.), shopkpr. 77 High st
°Birchall Alex. farmer, Sneyd villa, High st
Bird Jn. baker, 78 Church st
Blant Edwin, beer retlr. 103 High st
Bonnett Jn. Edwd. fishmngr. 9Church st
Bonsall Bros. grocers, 45 High st.
Bonsall Bros. nurserymen, Park rd
Bowers W. & Son, watch makers, 48 Church street
Brown Fred, shoe maker, 61 & 63 **High street**
Brown Geo. Edwin, shopkpr. 16 **Bridge st**
Burgess Caleb, shopkpr. 79 Victoria st
Burgess Geo. coal mer. 43 Kinsey st
Cliff Alphæus,yeast mer.124 Church st
Cliff Ronald L.R.A.M. teacher of **pianoforte, 124 Church st**
Cornwell T. C. Ltd. chemists & druggists, 52 & 54 Church st. T N 3
Cotterill Peter, confctnr. 50 Church st
Crown Inn (Geo. Dix), 16 Brook st
Cumberbatch W greengro 76 Church st
Dale Wm. insur. agt. 125 Church st
Davies Annie Mrs midwife, 33 High st
Deakin Arth. gents' hairdrssr. 126 **High st**
Deakin Jn.Thos.hairdrssr.7 Church st
Dean Fred, shopkeeper, 3 **Bridge st**
District Bank Limited (sub-branch) (open on tues. & fri. from 11 a.m. to 1 p.m.), 122 Church st.; head office, Spring gdns. Manchester
Downing Emily(Mrs.),grocer,3High st
Drill Hall (Danl.Jones,propr.),Park rd
Durber Jack, shopkpr. 12 Church st
East End Working Men's Club (Arth. Tunnicliffe, sec.), 11 Newcastle st
Edwards Lucy (Mrs.), shopkpr. 34 **Chapel st**
Embling Thos. florist, Abbey st
Fenton Wm. Thos. smith, High st
Fernyhough Saml. butcher, 62 **Church st**
Finnemore Jn. Wm. shopkpr. 24 Abbey st
Foresters' Arms P.H. (Mrs. Ann Louisa Mountford), 1 Cemetery la
Forrester Albt. Joshua, butcher, 55 **High st**
Freakley Jas. shopkpr. 3 Newcastle st
Globe Inn (Herbt.V.Beeston), 53 High st
Glover Alfd. billiards hall propr. 30 **High st**
Green Albt. Jn. blacksmith, Farmers bank, Abbey st
Green James, confectnr. 125 High st
Hall Jn.& Son, radiodlrs. 60 Church st.
Hall Albt. C. E. dentist, 206 High st
Hamner Geo.undertaker,Newcastle st
Hampton Wm. butcher, 14 Church st
Harding Edith Y. (Miss), tobccnst. 40 Church st
Harding Lavinia (Mrs.), hardware dlr. 38 Church st
Harrison Alfd. hairdrssr.57 Church st
Harrison Jsph. Thos. shopkpr. 4 & 5 Bridge st
Holden Ellen M. (Mrs.), cycle accessories dlrs. 85 **Church st**
Hough Jas. Alfd.printer,46 Church st
Ibbs Hilda (Mrs.), shopkpr. 146 Church st
Jackson Jsph. fried fish dlr. 37 **High st**
Jeavons Lilian (Miss), draper, 36 Church st
Johnson Percy Geo. M.B., Ch.B. physcn. & surgn. **The Bungalow,** Mill st. T N 49
Jones Hilda Ann (Mrs.), confctnr. 111 **Newcastle st**
Keay Wm. Edwd. shopkpr. 22 Vale Pleasant
Lee Bros. coal mers. 21 High st
Lee Jn. statnr. 28, & boot repr. 29, **Crown st**
Lowe John, grocer, 26 Church street
Lowndes Frank, pastrycook, 18 Church st
McCarthy Jas. fruitr. 45 Church st
Marsden Edwin,beer retlr.66Church st
Meakings Geo. smallholder, Spout House farm
Ministry of Labour Employment Exch. Methodist church, Newcastle st.
Minshull Mary E. (Mrs.), hardware dlr. 63 Church st
Morrall Geo.Thos.J.P.statnr.128 Highst
Mullineux J. S. & Son, butchers, 101 **Church st**
Mullineux Jsph.butcher,58 Church st
Mullineux Jsph.S. butcher, 42 Churchst
Nadin Mona Mrs, shopkpr. 22 Kinsey st
Norcup Saml. Ernest, gents' hairdresser, 84 Church st
Peake Wm Hy.grindery dlr. 30 Crown st
Pearl Assurance Co. Ltd. (Leslie W. Steele, district manager), Gordon ho. High st. T N 14
Pepper Clara (Mrs.), grocer 7Crown st
Phillips Bros. (Silverdale) Ltd. bldrs. May st. T N 63
Plim Eleanor E. Mrs butcher. 8 Crown st
Podmore Sarah (Mrs.), draper, 11 **Church st**
Rhodes Thos.fried fish dlr.79 High st
Roebuck P.H. (Jn. Hy. Bloor), 86 **Church st**
Rogers Saml. shopkpr. 35 **High st**
Roxy Cinema (A.Pico manager) High st.
Royal Oak Hot.(A.Cottrell), High st
Ryder Dudley, bldr. 106a. High st
Saunders Geo.H. butcher 94 Church st
Saunders Jack, draper, 56 Church st.
Scott Nellie Gwendoline (Mrs.), confctnr. 17 **Church st**
Shelton Iron, Steel & Coal Co. Ltd. colliery proprs. T N 22
Silverdale Aerated Water Co. Ltd. mineral water mfrs. Chapel st. T N 34
Silverdale Cemetery, Cemetery la
Silverdale Conservative Association & Club (Selwyn Healings, hon. sec.), 154 **Church st**
Silverdale & District Working Men's Club (Hy. Johnson, sec.) 29 Chapel st
Silverdale Equitable Industrial Cooperative Society Ltd. (Rt. Hulse, president; Nelson Gartside, sec. & manager), Crown st.; Victoria st. Kinsey st. & 30 Church st
Silverdale Social Service Centre (Jn. Reeves, sec.), High st
Silverdale Tileries Co. brick & tile mkrs. Silverdale tileries. T A "Silverdale Tileries, Silverdale, Staffs;" Silverdale 10
Simcock Geo. boot & shoe repr. 51 **Victoria st**
Skerratt Leonard, wine & spirit merchant, 90 **Church st. T N 19**
Smith & Morris, grocers, 65 High st.
Sneyd Arms (Harold Tilsley), High st
Southerton Herbt. poultry farmer, Red Heath
Star Inn (Mrs.Lily Evelyn Woodcock), 34 Church st
Steadman Jsph. wardrobe dlr. 73 **Church st**
Sutton Alfd. C. shopkpr. 18 Crown st
Swan Hotel (Jas. Taylor), 3 Mill st
Swettenhams Ltd. provsn. mers. 41 & 43 High st. T N 72
Timmis Alice Mrs grocer, 102 Church st
Turner Eli Fearn, beer retlr. Five Ways end, Vale Pleasant
United Tile Manufacturers, brick & tile mkrs. T N 10
Valco Goffredo, shopkpr. 3 Crown st
Vickers Nellie Miss shopkpr 148 High st
Viggars Elsie Mrs milliner, 22 Church
Viggars John, shopkeepr. 178 High
Vine Inn (Edwin Platt), 130 High st
Walley T. E. Ltd. tile mfrs. Rosemary Hill tileries. T A "Roofing, Silverdale;" T N 9
Ward Annie (Mrs.), hardware dlr. 33 Church st. T N 75
Watson J. & Son (Silverdale) Ltd. pawnbrkrs. 35 Albert st
Wedgewood Lizzie (Mrs.), shopkpr. 105 **Newcastle st**
Wheat Sheaf P.H. (Geo. Hazeldine), 129 Church st
White Harry, shopkpr. 88 Church st
White Horse Inn (Regnld. Shorthouse), 95 Newcastle st
Whittaker Mina (Miss), shopkpr.39a, High st
Wilkinson Thos.boot repr.107 Church st
Wilkinson Wm. fried fish dlr. 6 **Crown st**
Williams Thos. Olando, coal dlr 85 **Newcastle st**
Williams Wm.greengro.121 Newcastle st
Winkle F. E. registrar of births, deaths & marriages (mon. 1 to 2 p.m.), Methodist church, Chapel st
Woodcock Isabella (Mrs.), baker, 83 **High st**

Colliery complex. Here, filming was carried out using many of the colliery's employees as extras, including my late father Syd Bebbington. Yet film making being the deceptive trade that it is, Robeson never actually visited Silverdale, his part in long distance shots being undertaken by a local *miner. The Proud Valley* was as close a documentary as a film of the period could be, and is still regarded by some as the Welsh epic of the screen.

Daleians were indeed fortunate to have such lovely, interesting and contrasting countryside on their doorstep, and as children we revelled in the freedom of the woods and fields. Few areas can be bounded by such completely different types of scenery. The varied countryside close to hand is, to me, more interesting than flatter, less spoiled landscapes of some other English counties. I for one learned to appreciate the manifold beauty of this supposedly drab part of England at an early age, and have long considered Staffordshire to be a much underrated county by outsiders. Agreeing with these sentiments, the author and poet Charles Masefield in his classic work *Staffordshire* wrote that *'much of its scenery is beautiful, though comparatively few are aware of it'*. Walking in the area in my youth implanted in me a love of the countryside that has always been a continual source of delight and stimulation.

The author today outside his former birthplace in Chapel Street, Silverdale. *(Fred Hughes).*

Three
The Five Road Ends

Chapel Street, where I was born, virtually bisected the old village linking the main arteries of High Street and Church Street. In turn, Chapel Street itself was divided into two lengths by the Five Road Ends, so called because at this point there were junctions with Vale Street, Cross Street and Vale Pleasant. Some of my earliest memories are of playing with other local children of similar age at the Five Road Ends. With so little traffic at the time, we were safe although we were continually being told by parents to 'kapon the bricks!' (local dialect - keep on the bricks!). Having said that it was safe, I distinctly remember being in the company of my mother and witnessing a collision between, of all people, our local doctor in his car and a district nurse on her cycle!

In my childhood, the only lighting for the Five Road Ends was a gas column which stood on the footway outside Mr Burgess's house on the corner of Chapel Street and Vale Street. In the daytime the column would be used for various children's activities as part of their make believe world. It became the mast of a ship ploughing the high seas with someone climbing to the crow's nest, at other times, it might be swung upon with ropes and some girls even made use of it as a maypole. It was the centre of our universe. On no occasion in my childhood can I remember the lighting unit being vandalised.

Chapel Street, with its Staffordshire blue brindled brick pavements, dipped sharply from High Street to the Five Road Ends where two inspection covers were situated in the carriageway. From here, the rate of highway descent decelerated before levelling out for a short length and then the carriageway rose gradually to Church Street. Given that there was not the amount of traffic then, Chapel Street was our 'Cresta run' in the winter. In snow or icy conditions, the rate of descent from High Street was good for toboggans, or merely sliding on foot - unless you hit the inspection covers! Similarly, it was first-rate for cycling down, but if you hit the inspection covers, you were flying! The cycle tricks that youngsters attempt today, such as wheelies and flying, we were doing then - but not necessarily intentionally!

Due to its central location, the Five Road Ends played an important part in chapel anniversaries (or 'the charity' as the events were known locally). It was an essential stop for a burst of hymn singing by the parade of children from the relevant Sunday School who were generally accompanied by a band or, at the very least, a brass ensemble. On one such morning, the horse of our local milkman, Ruben Ford, was startled by the banging of a drum in nearby Brook Street. This resulted in churns being tipped from the cart into the highway and the milk flowing freely into nearby grids! Needless to say, Mr Ford was not too pleased! In our case, being from the Primitive Methodist Chapel (or 'The Prims' as it was affectionately known), we children were under the supervision of Sunday School Superintendent Joe Mothershaw, somewhat irreverently known as 'Holy Joe'. On weekdays Mr. Mothershaw could be found in the yard of local builders Philips Brothers in May Street. Previously he had been employed in the mining industry at the nearby Brymbo Colliery where he was a member of the Rescue Team. On occasions when an oratorio was being performed in the chapel, his marvellous bass voice could be heard booming from the choir stalls. The Five Road Ends was also the location for music at Christmas, generally provided by a Salvation Army Band or local chapel choir as they toured the village adding to the festivities.

For the most part, Chapel Street comprised modest terraced properties with privies and other facilities at the rear. Few were fortunate to possess gardens, although allotments were within a short distance for those with green fingers. Like most of the village housing stock, the properties were built in the 19th century, a number being intended to accommodate migrant workers who were seeking employment in the local mines and forges owned by the Sneyd family of Keele Hall. The deeds of our house were affixed with the Sneyd seal and, as a child, I recall my father wondering if at some future date the documents would be worth more than the house!

The rest of Chapel Street consisted of a mixture of development with the Bethel Chapel and Skerrett's wines & spirits shop being situated on either corner of the junction with Church Street. At the High Street junction, opposite corners were occupied by the Vine Inn and Morrall's newsagents respectively. On the west side of the street, the line of residential properties was broken by Edgar's shoe repairers, although the family lived over the shop. Also on this side, a brick-built air raid shelter protruded into the carriageway outside the Bethel Chapel. On the east side, Johnson's shop, Cotterill's taxi garage, Silverdale Aerated Water Company (or Brodie's Pop Works) and Skerrett's bottling stores interrupted the terrace of houses at intervals.

At the Five Road Ends itself, proceeding clockwise, the corner of Vale Street/Chapel Street was occupied by the residence of Mr & Mrs Burgess;

Edward's battery and accumulator charging shop was on the corner of Chapel Street/Cross Street; the Five Road Ends public house was located on the junction of Cross Street/Vale Pleasant, with the Working Men's Club (Top Club) opposite on the corner of Vale Pleasant/Chapel Street. Finally, Beech's general store stood on the other side of the road on the Chapel Street/Vale Street junction.

The Five Road Ends was a natural meeting place, where neighbours got together to gossip. But in the main, it was our domain, a playground virtually uninterrupted by traffic. The only vehicles likely to be seen in Chapel Street were those relating to the Pop Works, Skerrett's bottling stores and shop, Cotterill's taxi, a weekly Council refuse wagon or a horse drawn milk cart. There was little in the way of car ownership on the village at this period but, in any event, petrol was rationed. Otherwise the carriageway was ours and here a number of games were played. These had to be simple, there being little or no money, certainly nothing approaching the sophisticated gear of today. On our street there was plenty to keep us occupied - hopscotch, hide and seek, cowboys and indians, skipping, conkers, marbles etc. For the football season, jackets or coats were placed on the ground for goal posts, and wickets were chalked or painted on walls for cricket. There was a craze for collecting cigarette cards which was, in a way, educational. To possess a large collection was a status symbol and increasing it could become a major occupation.

On those occasions when the Council was undertaking road maintenance, we would watch fascinated at the giant steam roller which clanked and hissed as it flattened the new surface and, when the opportunity arose, the children would attempt to 'pop' the bubbles in the tarmac. This, of course, resulted in tar being deposited on hands and clothing which did not particularly find favour with parents! If a child was fortunate to possess a tricycle or bike, this would tend to have been handed down in the family, as would toys and clothes. Having parents who both came from large families, my relations ensured that I did not go short of anything.

Sometimes, with the aid of parents, 'bogies' would be constructed from planks of wood and pram wheels. Seated on this, the 'vehicle' was then steered with one's feet and a length of rope. Those children with a stronger imagination might, at times, convert the contraption into a tank using a box for the turret and a broom handle or short length of pipe for the gun. Occasional 'entertainment' was also provided by the arrival of brewers' drays at the Pop Works. At such times, we would stand and admire the skill of the drivers as they manhandled the heavy barrels from the vehicle, sliding them on a pair of portable rails onto bales of straw on the footway, before rolling them into the premises. Another welcome visitor was Mr. Hill, the village road sweeper who was like the Pied Piper to us children. A kindly gent, he allowed us to help him as he carried out his sweeping and we went with him into nearby streets. No doubt we were more of a hindrance than help to him, but he never actually gave us that impression. On other occasions, we could watch kitchen knives being sharpened in the street. This was accomplished with a small grindstone mounted on the handlebars of the trademan's bicycle. Today, this would no doubt receive the attention of the health and safety officials!

As we grew a little older and could be trusted out of our parents' eyesight, we were 'let out of harness' to play at the rear of the Five Roads End pub where some properties in Vale Pleasant had been abandoned following a Council Clearance Order just prior to the outbreak of war. This was a varied new playground offering an extraordinary selection of dens and camps to set ourselves up in. Also, having a friend who had grandparents in Eight Row, High Street, I was allowed to accompany him there and play in the communal open area to the rear which was accessed off Chapel Street.

At the end of Eight Row (next to the Roxy Cinema) was William Fenton's smithy. Here we could watch the blacksmith at work from a half open stable door, fascinating to us children, hearing the roar of the fire as he pumped up the flames before proceeding to craft a tool. And if we were lucky, he might be seen shoeing a horse from one of the local farms. As time went on we were allowed to venture even further afield where we revelled in the adjacent rolling countryside of the Jollies which rose over Gorsty Bank to Black Bank Road.

Situated to the rear of Church Street and a railway line which served the station and colliery, The Jollies comprised of an area of spoil mounds from earlier mining activity, allotments, but mainly Redfern's farm and associated fields. Said to have taken its name from The Jovial Colliers pub on Black Bank Road, the area to us children was a wonderful informal playground. We participated in football and cricket in season, then being a little older we progressed to what some might term 'a military type of activity.' Having seen films and newsreels about the war at the local cinema, we went in for handcrafted bows and arrows and catapults, and most streets had their own gang. These particularly came into their own in the Autumn around 5th November when raids might be made on a neighbouring bonfire structure, stripping it of the wood and transporting it to one's own. Empty railway wagons standing in the colliery sidings were also, at times, commandeered to become a fort, using the door as a drawbridge. Such activities might however be interrupted by a cry of 'Here's Andow!' Mr Andow was the colliery security man and whenever he appeared, we would beat a hasty retreat! Of course, we may have been pursuing mischievous pranks at times, but nothing vindictive nor vandalistic, otherwise, being in a tight community, our parents or, even worse the village policeman, might learn about it. Everyone knew everyone!

In the winter, our little gang's activities transferred indoors to premises at the rear of 107 Church Street, the residence of the Wilkinson family. The youngest son of Jim Wilkinson (or 'Clogger Jim'), Alan was an integral part of our group and many happy hours were spent, courtesy of his family, in a building principally used for storage of leather. This had the benefit of a stove and in this warm, safe environment numerous activities would take place on winter days, including our own, no doubt very amateurish, theatrical productions. Having girls in the group, we also played house and in doing so, learned to keep the premises tidy which came in useful in later life. At other times, I recall watching fascinated in the shop as Mr Wilkinson skilfully repaired miners' boots. In later years, this kind gentleman often repaired straps on my school satchel without charge, and no doubt did the same for other children.

There were many things we did at the time on the dale that no child should, perhaps, have been allowed to. We climbed trees, crossed a busy railway line (but not played on it!), paddled in streams or Jollies pool and felt mud between our toes whilst collecting newts or frogspawn, slid down slag heaps on a tin tray, had fights, and much more. Wearing shorts we came home with scratched knees or torn clothes and covered in mud but usually without broken limbs or serious injury. Seeing how children appear mollycoddled today for 'health and safety reasons' saddens me and makes one wonder whether we are creating a nation of softies or dependents, always needing to be protected. How will they learn to be independent, strong members of society, if they are overprotected?

Wartime advertisement for Mellards, a popular store in High Street, Newcastle, taking advantage of the Government's 'Dig for Victory' campaign.

BELOW:
Chapel Street with Skerrett's wines & spirits shop- photographed from its junction with Church Street by the late Harry Corfield just prior to demolition in the early 1950s. *(Hadgett Collection).*

Four
Living opposite the Pop Works

I was born at 15 Chapel Street, Silverdale, the son of Sydney and Alice Elizabeth Bebbington (nee Lavey). Raised in a loving, but strict environment, my father was employed as a blacksmith's striker at Kents Lane Colliery, the local mine.

Inclined to be parochial in outlook, villagers would perhaps have initially considered my mother to have been 'a foreigner' as she originated from Etruria where the majority of her family were employed in the pottery industry. As was generally the case at the time, my mother stayed at home during my early childhood and returned to 'the pots' when I was 8 or 9 years old. It was then relatively easy to regain employment on the pot banks as there were so many employers, many of them with famous names such as Wedgwood, Minton, Royal Doulton, etc. There was also a tendency for workers to move when news was gleaned of a wage increase at a neighbouring manufacturer. As a result, when my mother did return to full-time employment, she and her sister were employed by a number of pottery firms over a period of time.

There was no doubt who tended to dominate home life on the village, and this was the miners. In our house, it was my father who determined the character and stability of the home, and he maintained discipline. In contrast, my mother was a quiet, gentle and patient person, and the peacemaker. Generally, mining fathers were strict, and metered out punishment as necessary. No-one else was allowed to chastise his children with the exception, perhaps, of a schoolteacher or the village policeman. In the case of the latter, a cuff around the ear or even a boot up one's backside was considered acceptable, as you would have been deemed to have deserved it! Violence was not so widely condemned as today. A man's or parent's right to administer punishment was accepted. As children, we did not swear and men seldom allowed themselves more than a 'bloody' in front of women. Personally, I can not recall having heard my father swear at all. Children were deprived of familiarity with today's repetitious swear words in films and television programmes.

Chapel Street dwellings were the familiar Victorian terraced, two up, two down with front doors of the properties opening directly from the front room (or parlour) onto the brick footway. A number of the houses had an entry to the side which also provided rear access to other properties. Those entries which were covered were washed down regularly, and the majority whitewashed from floor to ceiling, but many were painted black or tarred on the bottom courses of bricks to a depth of approximately 1 foot. Outside privies also tended to share this style of dècor.

In my early childhood, our tile floored living room, or kitchen, was only covered with a peg rug. A high mantel fireplace occupied the majority of one wall, having an oven and hob on the right hand side and, on the opposite side, an iron rectangular boiler with a brass tap. These appliances, to my knowledge, were in all the neighbouring properties and no doubt fitted at the time they were built. Real coal fires cheered the long, dark evenings, much more comfortable than today's central heating. Brass handled toasting forks, crafted by my father, were used to toast slices of bread offered to the flames, then beef dripping thickly applied. Perhaps not considered as healthy eating today, but thoroughly enjoyed and it never seemed to do us any harm. Suspended from the ceiling in this room was the customary rack where freshly laundered items were aired. In my early days, clothes might also be aired on a guard placed in front of the fire.

In our case, the living room contained an important piece of equipment which was placed on the top of a chest of drawers - our Cossor valve radio. In its polished wooden case this was an essential tool in the pre-television days, and more so in wartime. It not only provided us with vital news information, but also entertainment which helped to boost the country's morale. It was a centre piece of life and the presenters and stars, such as Tommy Handley, Sandy Powell, George Formby, Harry Lauder etc., became treasured guests. Children's Hour was important to the young, but there was also programmes such as Happidrome (sic), ITMA, Workers' Playtime and concerts. ITMA (It's that man again!) was a particular favourite of mine, particularly as I grew older and learned to appreciate the humour of Tommy Handley and his team. The show had various characters whose catchphrases became part of our language: - 'I don't mind if I do' with which Colonel Chinstrap, played by Jack Train, turned any innocent remark into the offer of a drink; charlady Mrs Mopp (in real life Dorothy Summers) was always enquiring 'Can I do you now , sir?'; and never so cheerful Mona Lott could frequently be remarking 'It's being so cheerful that keeps me going!'. In its heyday, ITMA was said to have been heard by literally half the nation. It remained popular until Tommy Handley's death in 1949, having run for ten years.

They were social occasions sitting around the radio set, and on Saturday tea times, we had to be especially quiet to enable my father to listen to the sports results. At other times, if allowed, I would sit twiddling the half moon dial, catching voices speaking in foreign tongues from stations such as Hilversum, or Motala etc. Radio opened up the world for me and other children, and at an early age it helped me to appreciate classical music. As I grew up an important task was delegated to me, this being to take the acid filled accumulator to be recharged. Presumably, today, due to over protective health and safety legislation, I would not be able to carry out this simple task!

The front room tended to be used more for special occasions. This was carpeted and contained better quality furniture such as a sideboard, settee and chairs, an occasional table and even, perhaps, a piano. Best china and ornaments were kept in this room, assuming one had any, and possibly in a special cabinet.

Returning to the kitchen, a stairway led to two reasonable sized bedrooms, the rear one having a box facility. Under the stairwell was a lovely, cool pantry with a deep cellar where a well was understood to have been filled in. Here I played occasionally on my own if the weather was inclement, the area having natural light via a small window. As in the case of many of the village properties at the time, the bathroom was a tin bath which hung on a nail outside the rear door. This was a period when there was no pithead baths at the colliery and miners went home in their 'pit dirt.' As a consequence, most tin baths were in use daily. In fact, some of the older miners preferred to continue using them in preference to the colliery's pithead baths which were eventually installed after nationalisation. It has to be said, however, that the Victoria Colliery at nearby Biddulph had pithead baths in 1932.

Lighting of the houses was by gas which constantly fizzed, and during the war thick curtain material, or blankets, were hung over the inside of outer doors at night so that no source of light was available to enemy pilots. Also blackouts were installed over windows nightly for the same reason. These were generally homemade and comprised a wooden frame with a special material stretched over it. However, in the living room on winter nights, with the flickering of the fire on the ceiling and all this additional 'insulation', to me as a child, it was a lively, cosy atmosphere. We always had a good fire. We were fortunate in never being short of fuel due to colliery employees receiving a coal allowance.

In our rear yard was the outhouse, or back kitchen, where the paraphernalia of wash days was stored - a dolly, a galvanised tub and a fold down mangle with a table top, scrubbed white over the years. In addition, there was a brick sheathed corner boiler and a brown pitched sink with a single cold water tap. To the rear of the building was the privy and a large coal house. In the winter my father placed paraffin lamps in the toilet area to ensure that the system did not freeze in the low temperatures. Fancy toilet paper was not available, its equivalent during wartime being newspapers or the Radio Times cut into squares and hung on a nail with string. It was often said that in properties with an outside toilet, users had to have a long leg, or possess a good whistle!

Generally, the houses resembled little palaces inside. Outside the property, steps and footways would be swept and washed down daily together with the sills, to combat the dirt emanating from the chimneys of the colliery or local tileries. Some house-proud wives would use donkey stones which gave a good shine to the doorsteps. 'Doing the step' was a regular chore. Having a shiny step was paramount, and woe betide anyone who stepped on it before it was dry! It was also not unknown for washing to be done on more than one occasion in a day. If the wind was in the wrong direction, smuts would be deposited onto the freshly washed items drying on the lines stretched out in the rear yards. These would be gathered in, the whole process repeated and then re-hung outside again to dry.

In later years, the industrial chimneys were improved with filters, or demolished, thus alleviating the problem and, of course, improving the air. But in my childhood, certain activities in the street became associated with particular smells. For example, one could easily detect when it was washing day, or when bins were being emptied, they then contained ashes from the coal fires. In the winter, when snow or ice was on the ground, householders would spread ashes on the footways to prevent slipping, or even on the highway to keep vehicles moving.

We were most fortunate to have a garden at the rear of the house and on the other side of its hawthorn hedge was an orchard belonging to a property in Vale Street. This presented an open aspect. From my rear bedroom window I looked out over this, with the spire of St. Luke's Parish Church in the distance over the properties in Church Street. Like most families, we had an Anderson shelter in the garden, many of which were manufactured locally at Shelton Bar. This was a simple corrugated steel hut, 7.5ft long x 6ft wide in which to seek cover in the event of an air raid. It had a curved roof which was sunk 4ft into the ground and was, I understand, a DIY nightmare to assemble, not dissimilar to kits retailed today from certain major stores! A sheet of sacking, saturated with water and hung across the sandbagged doorway in the belief that it would

VERA LYNN

The songs

The first hit song of the war was *We're gonna hang out the washing on the Siegfried Line* which soon had a somewhat hollow ring as Hitler's armies swept towards the Channel. Arthur Askey's *Run, Adolph, run!* had people smiling again before long, and any song by Vera Lynn brought loved ones together—in their minds, if not in actuality.

The films

BING CROSBY AND INGRID BERGMAN

Gone With the Wind was the perfect antidote to wartime blues. It was the most popular film of the time. Who can ever forget the scheming Scarlett O'Hara flirting outrageously with Rhett Butler, and his gravel-voiced dismissal—"Frankly, my dear, I don't give a damn!" Another unforgettable film was the 1941 version of *The Philadelphia Story* starring Cary Grant, Katharine Hepburn and James Stewart. The Oscar winners of 1944 remained at the top of their professions all their lives. Bing Crosby played a singing priest in *Going My Way*, and Ingrid Bergman the persecuted heroine in *Gaslight*.

The theatre

Interesting to note that the most popular musical during the war was *Me and My Girl*, with Lupino Lane *Doing the Lambeth Walk*. It has had a tremendous success again in the current revival. Once a great musical, always a great musical . . .

"ME AND MY GIRL"

GLENN MILLER

The music

We danced to Glenn Miller's music—that beat was irresistible. But the end was tragic, when the maestro's plane mysteriously vanished into the sea on a wartime flight.

The books

More escapism! Yes, Margaret Mitchell's *GWTW* was the best-seller of the day, closely followed by an historical romp in somewhat similar vein—Kathleen Windsor's *Forever Amber*.

RICHARD DIMBLEBY

On the "wireless"

No one in Britain would willingly miss their weekly dose of laughter with *ITMA* (It's That Man Again!). The catchphrases of the irrepressible Tommy Handley and a cast of much-loved characters became part of everyday speech. An unexpected "star" emerged in Dr Charles Hill, the Radio Doctor, whose no-nonsense advice kept the nation fit and "regular"! Two other "household voices" were war correspondent Richard Dimbleby, and Alvar Liddell, whose reassuring tones announced the news, both good and bad.

TOMMY HANDLEY

ALVAR LIDDELL

The entertainers of the war period. The songs, the films, the music and the radio entertainers that kept morale high - 'till the blue skies drove the dark clouds far away.'

Rosemary Buildings with The Foresters Arms (or 'Corner Pin') left. Photographed by the late Harry Corfield prior to demolition in the early 1960s. *(Hadgett Collection).*

The Brighton Cottages, Silverdale. The railway signal box may just be seen to the left and the giant slag heap, often likened to an extinct volcano, in the background (*Barry Williams*).

My uncle, Les Bebbington, seen here in the lamp house at Silverdale Colliery. *(Author's collection).*

Children picking coal at Silverdale in the 1930s. *(Alan Scott).*

An early postcard of Kents Lane Colliery, Silverdale.

mitigate the effects of poison gas, contributed to an air of mustiness. Some 18ins of soil piled on top which soon sprouted plants or vegetables, gave the impression of an animal's burrow. The shelters were tense, gloomy places from which one emerged hobbit-like, stiff and tired after a night in the dark dormitory, to discover whether or not the family home had survived. I have a vague recollection of being carried into our shelter one night and remaining in there with my parents until the 'all clear' siren had sounded, but little else about the occasion. Other than that, I merely played in the place at times, but much preferred to be in the open air, as its atmosphere was not the most pleasant for a child. Public information leaflets such as *Your home as an air raid shelter* and *Air Raids - what you must know, what you must do* were issued by the Government and locally, the ARP was instructed to urge householders to erect their shelters immediately they received them.[1]

Times being what they were, the Government's 'Dig for Victory' campaign was publicly encouraged, the name being originated by the Evening Standard. Without doubt, it was the most successful home front initiative of the Second World War. Not only did it significantly reduce our reliance on imported food at a time when merchant ships were highly vulnerable to the deadly German U-boats, but it gave those not on active service, from the oldest to the youngest, the chance to feel they were making a vital contribution to the war effort. The campaign was launched with a high power publicity drive showing members of the Royal Family doing their bit with spade and hoe. Some public parks and school playing fields were rapidly converted into allotments, as was part of nearby Trentham Gardens. In turn, householders also ripped up treasured flower beds and lawns to grow vegetables. Regular horticultural advice was given on the radio and in newspapers by the Ministry of Information, typical examples being found in the *Staffordshire Advertiser* - 'Dig well to reap well' and 'Better tillage for top fields to maximise yield of crops'.[2] It was not unusual to find advice on other related matters in the press such as garden poultry keeping, control of water, beekeeping etc.[3]

The theory was that a plot of 90ft x 30ft could keep a family of five in vegetables all year round. Whilst not many may have managed that, by 1942 the Government estimated that more than half the families in Britain were growing at least some of their own food, and by the end of hostilities private gardeners were producing over a million tons of vegetables annually. My father, like many of his workmates, tended the garden and no doubt at times regarded this as a chore, particularly when on shift work. He was also liable to be called out on occasion, sometimes in the middle of the night, when a breakdown or emergency situation arose at the colliery. However, Dad provided as much in the way of vegetables as the garden would allow, a most useful addition to the family food. Home grown produce became the mainstay of many family meals, bulking out an increasingly restricted diet. Even garden hens were suddenly perceived as valuable assets! At the rear of the house we also had a couple of small areas of garden in the yard where my mother grew summer bedding. I learned to appreciate various varieties of flowers and gained an interest in gardening from an early age.

Some relations had allotments at The Acre site off Downing Street, or at the rear of Newcastle Street on the Jollies. Other sites were off Back Lane and opposite Rosemary Buildings and The Forrester's Arms (or 'Corner Pin') abutting the cemetery. As a child, I found allotments wonderful places to explore, the jumble of sheds and smoking stoves perhaps like a shanty settlement, but totally surrounded by thick hedges. The Acre site was a haven of peace, only interrupted by sounds of nature. In addition to growing vegetables and fruit, pigs were kept on some of the sites. These provided a cheap source of pork, bacon, ham, lard, suet and just everything else that could be obtained from the carcass. One delicacy was 'chitterlings' or pigs' intestines! Some men 'escaped' to allotments for such lengthy periods that their wives may have regarded themselves as gardening widows! On other allotment areas, the territory was shared with racing pigeon enthusiasts, a longstanding pastime on the village. With food rationing prevailing under the country's emergency powers, an unofficial system of bartering emerged, particularly at times of weddings or funerals, when families wished to make a good impression and to provide the best possible fare.

Times were tough, money short, and illness requiring a doctor could be a disaster. Benefits were scant, and there was no safety net of state funded family allowances and health care. However, the village was a tight community and generally no-one went without essentials, particularly the elderly. They always seemed to be the responsibility of their own relatives. There is not the same neighbourliness today on the new estates developed in the name of progress - the British way of life is a sadder society without it.

Notes

1) *Staffordshire Advertiser* 6th July 1940
2) Ibid 19th February 1944
3) Ibid 25th March 1944

Five
The price of coal

Mining has long been classed as one of the most difficult and dangerous forms of employment. It was generally carried out by men who had little choice but to work in the pits, and they were fortunate if they could survive without serious injury, respiratory disease or, worst of all, death. The common dangers and hazardous nature of the mining operations bound miners together in the dedication of performing their tasks, having in mind the safety of the whole colliery. They formed a comradeship the like of which is unlikely to be seen again, and this resulted in tight communities. Visiting a pub or workingmen's club, not only was it an education to be in their company but a privilege, and their sense of humour was unique. Men who could curse and swear mostly had gentle natures and could appreciate the finer things in life, such as art, literature and music. I've often heard it claimed that some of the miners, who came from all walks of life, were cleverer than academics, having been educated at the University of the Pit Bottom!

Being born and bred in a mining village, I regard miners as something special - a breed apart, or as local author Harold Brown called them 'most splendid of men.'[1] I grew up with the sound of miners' clogs on the pavements as shifts at the colliery changed. Through the generations, the mining industry produced first class workers, and only those who knew them or saw them at work will ever understand the skills with which they extracted coal from the bowels of the earth. Working conditions at times inevitably led to fatalities as may be witnessed from the memorial at the entrance to the village at Stonewall. Unveiled in 1996, the structure commemorates those whose lives were lost in the Silverdale mines. The names of 141 are recorded, but there are many who are not named. For example, those men from the village who died in other local mines such as Madeley, Leycett and Holditch. Also, those who suffered and died from respiratory diseases are also not named.

With the coming of World War II and around 3 million serving in the armed forces, mining and farming were among those occupations classed as 'essential or reserved' on account of not only having sufficient labour to produce the weapons and armaments, but also to maintain fuel supplies for the country. Those not eligible for active service were redirected into war related

My late father, Syd Bebbington (back row, 3rd from left & hatless), seen with colleagues outside fitting shops at the colliery. Early 1940s. *(Author's collection).*

Some of the colliery employees at a presentation for the retirement of Charles Brayford. *(Author's collection).*

occupations, and everyone that could possibly work was required to do so. This meant that both men and women were conscripted into war work, most notably the so called 'Bevin Boys'. From 1943, a ballot was taken of newly conscripted men, and one in ten of these was allocated to employment in the mines. In doing so, the Government acknowledged the importance of the coal mining industry at a most crucial stage of the war. Named after Ernest Bevin, then Minister of Labour, over 28,000 were diverted to fulfil this role.[2] Those in the Newcastle-under-Lyme area lived in billets or at a hostel in Knutton.

In another Government initiative to safeguard the industry, some 2,100 Newfoundland loggers were transported to Scotland to 'engage in the skilled work of cutting pit props', to replace foreign supplies no longer available.[3]

Even with the observance of secrecy and camouflage, some coalfields sustained aerial attacks from the Luftwaffe. Thus Silverdale's residents lived not only within the mournful sound of the air-raid siren in the centre of the village at Vale Pleasant, but also the powerful 'buzzer' at Kents Lane Colliery. Operated from the powerhouse, this device not only indicated times of the beginning or end of shifts, but also sounded continuously in the event of an emergency. Such an occasion arose in the early hours of Friday 3rd March 1944 when there was an ignition of firedamp in the colliery's underground No.2 District. Approximately 130 were underground when the incident occurred, 19 of whom were transferred to the North Staffs Royal Infirmary suffering from burns and shock. Of these, according to the press, 18 were detained for varying periods, but none were said to be *'very seriously injured'*.

At the time of the incident *'a loud report'* was said to have been heard *'followed by a flash, but no fire developed and the ignition was localised to the district in which it ignited.'* Rescue teams were not required, but first aid was administered underground. Work was stopped immediately at the colliery as a precautionary measure before being declared 'fit for work' following an underground investigation led by Mr John Walker, the General Manager, and his officials. One of the miners transferred to hospital later died from his injuries, having received *'extensive burns to the face, arms and body'*. He was later named as 57 year old Joseph Burke, a colliery packer, of 23 Downing Street. His death was subsequently the subject of an inquest by H.M. Coroner.[4]

By coincidence, in the same edition of the *Sentinel* in which the unfortunate death of Joseph Burke was reported, figures were given of national coal productivity. Output of saleable coal was given as 3,769,000 tons per week, an increase of 273,500 tons over the preceding 4 weeks. The percentage of standard tonnage from North Staffordshire was given as 89.3%.[5]

Competition between coalfields developed out of pride in performance. Yet beyond this was a common bond - a fellow loyalty born out of shared experience. Kents Lane Colliery had an excellent record of productivity and in later years I can recall seeing the target flag flying proudly from the mast on the top of the pithead gantry. In fact, in the street it would be a topic of conversation. Again it was a matter of pride and rightly so.

One of those injured in the incident of March 1944 was Stanley Flynn, then in his early twenties. The Flynns were a well known and respected family living next door but one to us in Chapel Street. Their daughter Dorothy was one of my street gang of playmates. Times being what they were and the village being a tight community, friends and neighbours rallied around the Flynn family assisting where they could, or at the very least paying a call at the house to enquire about the condition of Stan who was the eldest of the four children. I can recall being taken by my mother on a number of occasions to visit 'the patient' who was usually lying in the front room. Given that contemporary press reports state that, apart from the deceased miner, none of the others who were detained in hospital were 'very seriously injured', I nevertheless recollect being shocked at the extent of some of the burns which were evident on Stan's body. Stan did eventually return to work at the colliery but, according to the family, burn marks were still visible all over his body when he died in 1994 - some fifty years after the accident.[6]

It was only after nationalisation of the industry in 1947 that safety standards were regulated. Before this, each pit was as 'safe' as the individual owners cared to make it. However, even after nationalisation, coal mining remained a hazardous job, and fatalities and injuries were a fundamental part of it. Such is the price of coal!

Notes

1) Harold Brown. *Most Splendid of Men* (Blandford Press).
2) David Day. *The Bevin Boy* (Ashford, Buchan & Enright. Leatherhead).
3) *Staffordshire Chronicle* 6th July 1940.
4) *Staffordshire Advertiser* 4th & 11th March 1944.
5) *Sentinel* 4th March 1944'
6) Dorothy Ellam (nee Flynn). Letter to author 6th April 2006.

Six
Bevin Boys

Millions were directed into unfamiliar and unpleasant work during World War II. Among these were some 28,000 young men who collected a pit helmet and miners' lamp instead of a uniform. These individuals became known as Bevin Boys. Named after Ernest Bevin (1881-1951), then Minister of Labour & National Service, the Bevin Boy scheme involved one out of every ten young males available for the armed services being conscripted into mining - the country's hardest and most dangerous industry. This resulted from the war effort being in danger of grinding to a halt in 1943 because of the lack of coal, the government having short-sightedly allowed thousands of miners to enlist into the forces at the outbreak of war. In addition, the pits were losing 20,000 annually through retirement, death, long-term illness and disablement. Recruitment was not keeping pace with natural wastage.

It came as a shock to those concerned on receiving the anticipated OHMS envelopes to learn that, instead of fighting for their country, they were being sent into the coalmines! Bevin Boys came from all walks of life, and those originating from mining areas generally trained locally. Others from non-mining parts of the country could be sent anywhere initially. After training, they could theoretically chose where to work, but without a guarantee of actually being posted there. Most living in mining communities chose to work at a local pit meaning that they could remain at home, thus taking pressure off scarce accommodation. However, in practice, this did not always work out, with lads from the south being posted to the north and vice versa! In North Staffordshire, Fenton's Kemball Colliery was established in 1942 as the first training centre for boys entering the mining industry, and this became part of the government network of training centre collieries. In addition, some classes were held at the North Staffordshire Technical College.

The arrival of the Bevin Boys in North Staffordshire presented a number of problems to the authorities, particularly billeting officers. Already overworked, having had to find accommodation for evacuees and service personnel arriving in the area, plus hundreds of bank staff from London destined for the Central Clearing House at Trentham, they struggled to find lodgings for the young conscript miners. As a consequence, a number of the lads initially found themselves billeted at such places as Frobisher Hall at Mill Meece, one of the halls of residence specially built for the munitions workers at the nearby Royal Ordnance Factory, Swynnerton.

However, it has to be said that there were also problems for the friendly invaders themselves, as some had difficulty in understanding the language! Those who originated from the north tended to fare the best, but those from the south could have perhaps benefited from a phrase book such as a copy of the later *Arfur Tow Crate in Staffy Cher*. As it was, they had to rely purely on the natives for translations, for example - 'Whut dust mane, yooth?' - 'what do you mean, youth?' When the miners slipped into their own dialect, some Bevin Boys were completely lost. The miners would talk to each other at times, and the newcomers would not always realise that they were being lampooned.

Initially 'foreigners' had to learn that 'duck' was a local form of endearment and also to listen carefully to bus conductors' destination calls eg. 'Anlyonly!'was Hanley or Hanley only. Other noticeable examples of destinations that they had difficulty in understanding were 'Boslem!' - Burslem, and 'Bow Grain' - Ball Green. But if the miners and locals' ways of talking seemed odd to the Bevin Boys, so did the speech of the Bevin Boys to the miners, especially those highly educated ones conscripted from London and the south of England. The late Fred Leigh in his book *Most Valiant of Men* wrote of a parson's son from London who on arrival at Norton one morning said 'I say, it's frightfully cold this morning'. A collier responded 'Eh surry. Whot didst see?' The lad repeated 'it's frightfully cold this morning'. The collier replied 'Ah, ah'll 'ave ter practice that!' On another occasion at a local colliery, a Bevin Boy was instructed to phone the Under-Manager because an item of equipment had stopped working. After a brief conversation the lad was told to get off the phone and get someone 'who could speak b..... English!'

The miners would remark with a smile 'wot's they on abite yooth?' North Staffordshire people, and Daleians in particular, have a keen sense of humour, but it is of a dry variety which may not be appreciated by those from outside the area. Coupled with this, there is a wealth of humour amongst miners themselves, even underground and in dangerous conditions. For example, a low beam or girder below ground at one local colliery was marked 'Duck or Grouse!' Daleians have the ability to tell a joke with an innocent, straight face, finally leaving those listening with the realisation that they have been taken for a ride! But, after a while and working together, most of the Bevin Boys began to understand the humour of the area and appreciate the camaraderie. On occasion the Bevin lads and the miners would even attempt to mimic each other!

The social life in the area during World War II was described as 'pretty hectic' and the Bevin Boys found it very much to their liking. In addition to the 'local talent', vast numbers of female workers were present, away from home, being employed in munitions and other factories. These could be found at venues where dances were regularly held including the Municipal Hall and Castle Hotel in nearby Newcastle-under-Lyme. In addition, Spooners, (or The Silver Slipper) a small dance hall off Silverdale's High Street, was a popular haunt which attracted local American service personnel. Long-time friend Brenda Kitching informed me that, on occasion, famous popular bands or groups of the time could be found playing there, one she particularly recalls being the Ray Ellington Quartet.

Additional competition for the girls came from members of the Fleet Air Arm based at Clayton Hall and members of the American armed forces based at Keele Hall, Crewe Hall and Nelson Hall, Cotes Heath. From time to time, this gave rise to rivalries which exploded into physical violence on a significant scale. Tensions often erupted between the parties, disagreements generally being about girls, and due to too much alcohol. Misunderstandings could also arise merely as a result of differences in the meaning of language! Pitched battles would commence in a Newcastle pub and spill over into the town centre with participants armed with bricks, bottles and just about everything which came to hand. The civilian police usually could not handle the situation and peace was only restored with the arrival on the scene of both American military and Royal Navy police patrols. For their part, the American military police - the notorious 'Snowdrops' (so called because of their white helmets) - were renowned for their use (or misuse!) of batons - generally, one did not argue with them. Sometimes the fracas was so serious that participants were hospitalised and some hostelries such as the Talbot and the Smithfield were declared out of bounds for periods.

Former Bevin Boy Jack Russell was not involved in any such activities and did not recall witnessing any fighting. Born in London, he initially had a medical examination with a view to joining the Royal Navy, but was then surprised and disappointed to find that he was being diverted into the mines! Trained at Askern Main Colliery, near Doncaster, at the age of 18, he was then transferred to Silverdale Colliery. On arrival in the area, accommodation was scarce which resulted in him and thirteen others being billeted at Frobisher Hall, Mill Meece. Here he found the social life 'wonderful', particularly with

Warwick Taylor MBE, Vice-President of the Bevin Boys' Association on the right, at a reunion at Apedale Heritage Centre. *(Staffordshire Archives).*

A 1930s view of Silverdale Colliery. *(Basil Jeuda).*

sharing the same block as some of the female munitions workers who were employed at the nearby Royal Ordnance Factory, Swynnerton. One of Jack's colleagues was a ballroom dancer who organised regular dancing lessons at the hall of residence. He fondly recalls attending these popular events and never being short of partners.

Jack spent six months at Frobisher Hall, being transported daily into Silverdale by special coach. After this time, he was transferred to Knutton Miners' Hostel where he found life 'comfortable'. The staff were 'very good' he recalls, and they provided him with 'snappin' (sandwiches) to take with him to work. From Knutton he walked to the mine, crossing the Jollies fields and then via the railway line into the colliery complex. At the time he was at the pit he believes that there were five other Bevin Boys employed. He himself worked on haulage at the pit bottom which he says involved *'keeping your wits about you!'* Although he witnessed a number of serious accidents, he *'liked the work and enjoyed the camaraderie.'* As he put it - *'you went into the mine a boy, and came out a man!'* It should also be noted that Jack wore spectacles which was uncommon for miners. At some collieries, those wearing glasses were considered a risk and found work on the surface.

Many of the Bevin Boys became mates with their mining colleagues and socialised with them, going to pubs to have a drink and perhaps play dominoes, darts or cribbage. Jack was no exception and frequented the Old Pomona Inn on Newcastle's Lower Street with some of the miners from the colliery. He also enjoyed their company at local football matches at the former Victoria Ground in Stoke, particularly when Stanley Matthews was on the pitch.

Jack was forced to leave the colliery after a year on account of deteriorating eyesight.[1] He was certainly not the only Bevin Boy who was eventually found to be medically unfit for work in the mines. Among these was Eric Bartholomew who had to be discharged from a colliery at Accrington. Later to find fame as comedian Eric Morecambe, he was diagnosed to have a heart condition from which he was to die in middle age. In a radio interview former Bolton and England footballer Nat Lofthouse claimed that having been a Bevin boy was *'one of the best things that could have happened to him'*. As a result of pushing tubs, his body became 'firmer and harder' and his legs 'stronger' thus enabling him to shoot 'with much greater power.'

Fit or otherwise, some conscripts could not cope with the heat, noise or dust of the underground. Feeling claustrophobic, they never got used to the 'dark closed-in feeling.' Some, whilst attempting to do their best and pull their weight, were simply unfit or incapable of carrying out mine work.

As to the actual number of Bevin Boys who would have been employed at Silverdale, no records survive. In any event, many coalmining records were lost in the transfer of the industry from colliery owners to the Coal Board upon nationalisation in 1947. However, according to Warwick Taylor MBE, Vice President & Chairman of the Bevin Boys Association, it is unlikely that many would have been employed at Silverdale. They tended to be employed at the larger pits where miners exceeded 1,500. In 1944/45, Silverdale had only 805 miners (working surface and underground). The number of conscripts who went into the Midlands coalfields, including Staffordshire, during World War II is believed to have been in excess of 4,000.[2]

Britain's war effort never stalled because of the shortage of coal. By taking over certain jobs such as haulage at the collieries, Bevin Boys freed up regular miners to work at the coalface. At some collieries, those Bevin Boys who were capable of doing so, did actually work on the coalface. The last Bevin Boys were released from service in 1948. Since that time the question of a medal for their service has arisen but it was not until 1995 that their contribution was first officially acknowledged in speeches to mark the 50th anniversary of VE Day by the then Prime Minister John Major and Her Majesty the Queen. Finally, in 2007 after a lengthy campaign, the government announced that the Bevin Boys were to be awarded a Veterans' Badge.

At the time of writing, a campaign is underway by the Bevin Boys Association to create a permanent memorial at the National Memorial Arboretum at Alrewas to honour the thousands of conscripts who worked in the mines during World War II. As Councillor Ross Irving, Leader of Stoke-on-Trent City Council in adding his support to the campaign stated - 'many had no mining experience or knowledge, but they worked to fuel this country when it was needed most.'[3]

Notes

1) Letter to author 6th October 2009 and subsequent telephone interviews.
2) Letter to author 15th December 2009.
3) City Council press release 8th October 2009.

Seven
Waste not, want not!

During my childhood the term 'recycling' probably did not exist. Not that we were in anyway wasteful, because during the dark days of the Second World War, everything that could be re-used, most certainly was!

While there was no official rationing until 8th January 1940, the consequences of the German U-boat campaign against Britain's Atlantic convoys resulted in an early effect on consumers. For example, imported luxury items became scarce and rapidly disappeared from the shelves. Also, home production of everything deemed to be 'inessential' ceased as manufacturing was transformed to produce munitions. Conserving of metal then became crucial. Wrought iron railings, some of it historic, was removed from the front of public buildings, churches, etc to be converted into weapons of war, and everyone was encouraged to collect material such as aluminium, tin baths, tin cans and old saucepans for recycling.

In the home almost everything that crossed the threshold was re-used at least once, including the tea leaves in some households, and then scattered onto the garden to be dug in as fertiliser. Sardine tins would be mopped up thoroughly with a crust of bread, cake mixture bowls licked clean and piccalilli jars prodded until there was nothing more for a fork to spear! Remnants of household fires would be riddled and cinders reburnt. The remaining ash was then spread on the garden for fertilising, as was soot following a visit from the chimney sweep. However, with Silverdale being a mining village, the practise of reburning cinders was not so prevalent on account of miners having a coal allowance.

Collecting of salvage became a focus of the war effort, practised in the home or by clubs and youth organisations. Salvage generally comprised waste paper, tins and glass. This would be placed in suitable containers for collection by the Council on alternate weeks to the emptying of bins. Unlike today, salvage collection was done using an ordinary refuse collection vehicle. On arrival at the Council's depot in Newcastle-under-Lyme, the waste paper was baled and then collected on a regular basis by Thames Board Mills of Warrington. According to Eric Warrillow, former Director of Housing & Health, the company also supplied the baling machine to the local authority.

But, times being what they were with no luxury toilet paper available, some newspapers or magazines were retained by householders for use as toilet paper. Other publications might be donated to the local 'chippie'. Some villagers contended that fish and chips never tasted better than when wrapped in pages of the *Sentinel*.

At the Council depot, tins were baled and collected by a recovery company. Glass was also sorted into various types and colours and any bottles sent to a local bottle recovery service where they were cleaned and returned to the company of origin. Many of the beer, wine and pop bottles had a small cash deposit charged on purchase to ensure their return, whereupon the deposit would be refunded. As a result, the majority were returned, some having been collected by children to boost their pocket money. Empty bottles might be given to youngsters as a reward for having run an errand, so they could redeem the deposit.

Some discarded clothing would be put out for the rag and bone man who appeared regularly on the village with his horse and cart. Other material such as old curtains and pillowcases would be cut up for dusters and teacloths. Wool was also carefully unravelled from defunct pullovers and refashioned into other items of clothing. As for anything else in the used clothing line such as shirts, vests, coats and even blankets - they were put to one side to be 'clipped.' This was generally a practise reserved for winter nights around the fireside with the family cutting up the discarded items into 6 inch strips approximately 1.5 inches wide. These would eventually be embedded with a special tool into a sheet of hessian, or a former sugar bag begged from the local Co-op store - it was not unknown for there to be a waiting list for these. After many hours of labour, a magnificent clip or 'pegged' rug to rival Joseph's coat of many colours was produced !

Tiny kitchens often doubled as workshops or tool sheds with people having to 'make do and mend'. Men seemed to have an impressive armoury of tools such as hammers, pliers and spanners. It was not unusual for a baby's cot to be constructed from timber formerly an old drawer. Children's clothes were created from worn out adult clothing and all manner of inventive solutions were found to replace things in short supply. Whilst the village had a number of cobblers, a few households owned an authentic last which ensured savings on at least minor shoe repairs. At that period, no-one appeared to go barefoot!

In my childhood, milk was delivered by horse and float. My impression was that the large gentle creatures needed little or no control, knowing the route and where to stop as well as the milkman. On hearing the sound of horse's

DIET for a child from 12 to 17 years MENU

One food from each of the sections (*a*), (*b*), (*c*), (*d*), etc., below should be served at each meal.

BREAKFAST 8.0 - 8.30 a.m.

(*a*) Whole-grain cereal.—1-2 cupfuls of: porridge, or wheatmealies, or wheatflake preparations, or stewed fruit (in hot weather) with milk.
(*b*) An egg, fresh or dried (twice a week), or bacon with 2-4 oz. potato, or 1-2 oz. bread, or fish (once a week) (herrings tinned or fresh if possible).
(*c*) National bread.—2-4 whole slices as: toast with
(*d*) Butter.—2-3 teaspoons, or margarine, or dripping, or bacon fat.
(*e*) Cocoa or tea to drink.

MID-MORNING 10.0 - 11.0 a.m.

Milk—½ pint (if at school).

DINNER 12.30 - 1.0 p.m.

(*a*) Meat, fish or cheese, etc.—2-3 tablespoons of: beef or mutton, or liver or kidney, or brains, or sweetbread, or chicken, or rabbit, or fish (fresh, salt or dried), or cheese (1-2 tablespoons), or dried egg (one).
(*b*) Cooked fresh vegetables.—2-3 heaped tablespoons of cabbage or greens, or cauliflower, or spinach, or sprouts, or swedes, or parsnips, or carrots, or fresh peas or beans.
(*c*) Potatoes.—3-4 heaped tablespoons.
(*d*) Pudding.—3-4 tablespoons of milk pudding, or blanc-mange, or fruit or sweet tart or flan, or steamed pudding, or baked pudding, or stewed fruit and custard, etc.
(*e*) National bread.—1-2 whole slices or extra potato.
(*f*) Water to drink.

NOTE.—Dried peas, beans or lentils should be added to the meat, fish or cheese portion, if a full serving cannot be obtained through rationing or shortage.

TEA 4.30 - 5.0 p.m.

(*a*) National bread.—3-6 whole slices with:—
(*b*) Butter.—2-3 teaspoons, or margarine, or dripping with:—
(*c*) Raw salad, or raw shredded vegetable, or vegetable sandwich filling.
(*d*) Cake.—1-2 slices, or rusks or biscuits.

SUPPER 7.0 - 8.0 p.m.

(*a*) Pulse vegetable dish, or cheese, or fish with:—
(*b*) Cooked fresh vegetables.—2-3 heaped tablespoons (see dinner), or salad with:—
(*c*) Potatoes.—3-4 heaped tablespoons.
(*d*) National bread.—2-4 whole slices with:—
(*e*) Butter or margarine.—2 teaspoons with:—
(*f*) Jam, or syrup, or vegetable yeast extract, or paste.
(*g*) Soup, cocoa or milk drink.

BREAKFAST

1st Day—Porridge and milk; egg; toast and butter; tea.
2nd „ —Wheatmealies and milk; bacon and fried potato; toast and butter; tea.
3rd „ —Porridge and milk; fish cakes; toast and butter; tea.
4th „ —Wheatmealies and milk; bacon and fried bread; toast and butter; tea.
5th „ —Porridge and milk; bacon and potato cakes; toast and butter; tea.
6th „ —Wheatmealies and milk; scrambled dried egg; toast and butter; tea.
7th „ —Porridge and milk; savoury potato cakes; toast and butter; tea.

DINNER

1st Day—Roast joint; cabbage and roast potatoes; chocolate mould; national bread or extra potatoes.
2nd „ —Vegetable pie; cauliflower or parsnips and jacket potatoes; baked sponge pudding; national bread or extra potatoes.
3rd „ —Braised liver or beef; mashed swedes and boiled potatoes; milk pudding and jam; national bread or extra potatoes.
4th „ —Cheese pudding or lentil cutlets, or sausage and bean pie; sliced carrots and mashed potato; baked apple or stewed fruit and custard (or bread pudding); national bread or extra potatoes.
5th „ —Shepherd's pie; greens and potatoes; ginger pudding and custard; national bread or extra potatoes.
6th „ —Lancashire hot-pot; peas (or sprouts or spring greens); trifle; bread or extra potatoes.
7th „ —Brown rabbit stew (or steak and beans); spinach (or greens) and potatoes; chocolate duff; national bread or extra potatoes.

NOTE.—Mock cream may be served with puddings.

TEA

1st Day—Parsley and potato sandwiches; sweet biscuits; tea.
2nd „ —Toast and butter; home-made cake; tea.
3rd „ —Bread and jam; biscuits; tea.
4th „ —Spinach (raw) and cheese sandwiches; sweet biscuits; tea.
5th „ —Bread and jam; home-made cake; tea.
6th „ —Cheese, pickle and raw cabbage sandwiches; sweet biscuits; tea.
7th „ —Carrot and parsley sandwiches; cake; tea.

SUPPER

1st Day—Vegetable and cheese sauce and potatoes; national bread and jam; cocoa or soup.
2nd „ —Sardine salad and jacket potatoes; sweet rusks; cocoa or soup.
3rd „ —Potato cheese, national bread and butter; watercress (or cabbage) salad; cocoa or soup.
4th „ —Haricot beans on toast; carrots and potatoes; national bread and jam; cocoa or soup.
5th „ —Cheese, jacket potatoes; mustard and cress and spinach salad; national bread and butter; sweet wheatmeal rusks; cocoa or soup.
6th „ —Pulse soup or pulse dish and potato; national bread and jam; cocoa. (Pulses are dried peas, beans and lentils.)
7th „ —Cauliflower cheese or cheese salad, jacket potatoes; sweet rusks; cocoa or soup.

Ministry of Food leaflet (The Second World War Experience Centre).

Christmas Pudding

2 oz. plain flour
½ level teaspoon baking powder
½ level teaspoon grated nutmeg
¼ level teaspoon salt
¼ level teaspoon cinnamon
1 level teaspoon mixed spice
2–4 oz. suet or fat
3 oz. sugar
½–1 lb. mixed dried fruit
4 oz. breadcrumbs
1 oz. marmalade
2 eggs, fresh or dried
¼ pint rum, ale, stout or milk

Sift flour, baking powder, salt and spice together. Add the sugar, fruit and breadcrumbs and grated suet or melted fat. Mix with the marmalade, eggs and rum, or other liquid. Mix very thoroughly. Put in a greased basin, 2 pt. size. Cover with greased paper and steam for 4 hours. Remove the paper and cover with a fresh piece and a clean cloth. Store in a cool place. Steam 2 to 3 hours before serving. The steaming is best done by standing the basin in a saucepan with water coming a third of the way up the sides of the basin. Keep the water boiling gently over a low heat. It may be necessary to add a little more water during cooking but be sure the water is boiling when added.

Christmas Cake

3 oz. sugar
4 oz. margarine
1 level tablespoon syrup
8 oz. plain flour
2 level teaspoons baking powder
Pinch of salt
1 level teaspoon cinnamon
1 level teaspoon mixed spice
2–4 eggs, fresh or dried
1 lb. mixed fruit
½ teaspoon lemon substitute
Milk to mix

Cream sugar and margarine, add syrup. Mix flour, baking powder, salt and spices together. Add alternately with the egg to the creamed mixture and beat well. Add fruit and lemon substitute and enough milk to make a fairly soft consistency. Line a 7" tin with greased paper, put in the mixture, and bake in a moderate oven for two hours.

Mincemeat

½–¾ lb. mixed dried fruit
4 oz. apples or 2 ozs. apple rings
3–4 oz. sugar
2–4 oz. suet or melted margarine
2 level tablespoons marmalade
½ level teaspoon mixed spice
½ level teaspoon cinnamon
1 level teaspoon grated nutmeg
¼ level teaspoon salt
4–6 tablespoons, rum, sherry, stout or ale
½ level teaspoon lemon essence
Few drops rum essence—optional

A MINISTRY OF FOOD LEAFLET

For method see over the page

Ministry of Food leaflet (The Second World War Experience Centre).

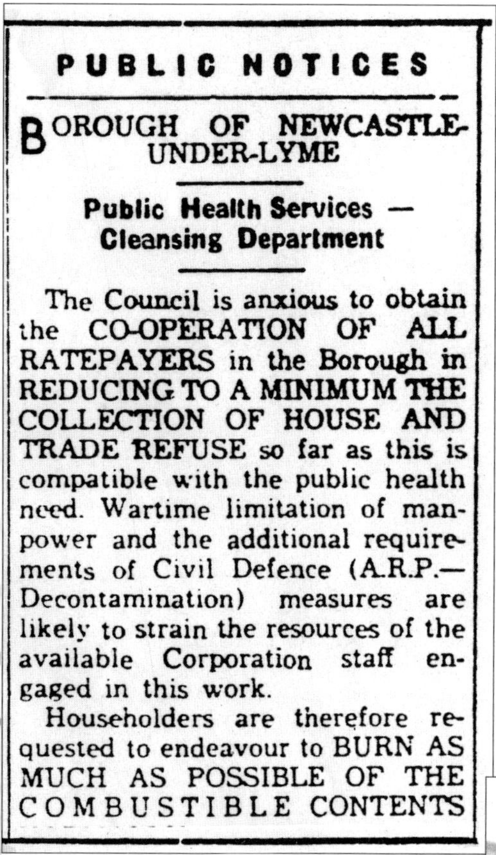

PUBLIC NOTICES

BOROUGH OF NEWCASTLE-UNDER-LYME

Public Health Services — Cleansing Department

The Council is anxious to obtain the CO-OPERATION OF ALL RATEPAYERS in the Borough in REDUCING TO A MINIMUM THE COLLECTION OF HOUSE AND TRADE REFUSE so far as this is compatible with the public health need. Wartime limitation of man-power and the additional requirements of Civil Defence (A.R.P.—Decontamination) measures are likely to strain the resources of the available Corporation staff engaged in this work.

Householders are therefore requested to endeavour to BURN AS MUCH AS POSSIBLE OF THE COMBUSTIBLE CONTENTS

Wartime public notice of September 1939.

Wartime poster promoting frugality in the kitchen. *(Author's collection).*

Eli Bagguley on his allotment at Rosemary Buildings. *(Mary Clews).*

The former Smith & Morris store on the junction of High Street/May Street seen in wintry conditions (from *Life on the Dale* by Barry Williams).

Victoria Street, Silverdale with the large Co-operative premises on the left. The rooms over the two shops were the venue for many functions like wedding receptions. (From *Life on the Dale* by Barry Williams).

hooves on the carriageway, there would be a 'twitching of curtains.' This might be followed by the 'manure Olympics' with householders rushing to the door with bucket and shovel in the hope of gaining some rich source of fertiliser. If this transpired, it was amusing to see the race to secure the 'deposit' (or 'hoss muck' to Daleians) which was eventually recycled on the garden. This, together with soot and ash helped in the 'Dig for Victory' campaign but in any event, there were not the variety of fertilisers available at the time from horticultural merchants. In return for leaving a 'deposit' a crust of bread or fallen apples would be given to the horse as a reward.

Householders were also encouraged to save food waste to help feed pigs and other livestock. There was less pressure in this respect, however, as the population could not afford to waste food. Pig swill mainly resulted from chip shop waste and collection was generally private. However, some local authorities did install galvanised bins at street corners where food waste could be left for collection. This was then minced, boiled , sterilised and compressed into cake-like lumps, then watered down and fed to pigs who seemed to relish it. No-one appeared to suffer any dreadful diseases as a consequence, nor were there any epidemics among pigs, but I presume that present regulations would not allow such a scheme.

At Silverdale there was a 'special' alternative method of collection of waste in the form of Bob Harrison (1903-1981). To us children, Bob resembled Biggles, the character from Captain W.E. Johns' popular books; he appeared on the village wearing a World War I type flying helmet and a large leather coat. He thundered into Silverdale astride a powerful old Norton motorcycle attached to which was a large homemade box built onto the original sidecar chassis. This was used to collect swill for his pigs. But there was far more to Bob Harrison than the simple, but jovial farmer he appeared. According to John Belcher, former Colliery Manager at Silverdale, Bob had a natural instinct for geology although he had no formal training. A direct descendant of an original Klondike gold prospector, he was very knowledgeable about local coal seams and outcrops, and top mining engineers called upon his uncanny ability to detect hidden coal measures and to help them survey the district's coal deposits.

Bob and his wife Catherine Millicent lived a simple existence at Bank Top Farm, a 19 acre holding near Crackley. The home was lit with a single bulb powered from a car battery which was regularly recharged with the generosity of the management of the local colliery. The late Don Rogerson had happy memories of Bob whom he described as a big man with a crop of white curly hair. He and his wife were lovers of classical music and, at times, this was evident with the sound emanating from a wind-up gramophone heard over the local countryside on summer evenings. When he died on 28th December 1981, pitmen from all over North Staffordshire attended his funeral at Keele.

I've often heard it said that times of adversity bring out the best in the British. The process of recycling as it was then, and collection of salvage are typical examples. Salvage drives encouraged the feeling of contributing directly to the war effort, and it was this attitude spurned on by the stirring speeches of Churchill and Priestley, that helped gain victory.

Farmer and geologist Bob Harrison.
(Claude Hadgett).

Wartime poster.
(Stephen Garnett, Editor of This England).

Eight
Food & Rationing

Coping with everyday life during World War II was far from easy and yet us children, not able to grasp the situation and possible danger, seemed to revel in all the fuss. Food, petrol and clothes were rationed, not to mention soap. No one was allowed to have a bath of more than 5 inches of water, although precisely who enforced this particular regulation escapes me. I certainly cannot recall any official with a ruler visiting us on bath nights!

Although often irksome, Britain's strict food rationing system had its compensations. For example, the standard food ration was devised by experts, in particular Professor R.A. McCance, to help ensure that the whole population was well fed, whilst discouraging wholesale civilian indulgence in any form of gluttony. Also, the system 'forced' housewives to draw on their culinary ingenuity, learning to cook some of the things that they would never have dreamed of attempting to serve up before the war - sheep's head, fruit cakes made with dried eggs and grated beetroot, 'banana' sandwiches made from parsnips flavoured with artificial brown flavouring, carrot marmalade etc.

Strictly controlled prices were introduced in the hope of avoiding profiteering, but some shopkeepers kept un-rationed goods 'under the counter' for favourite or regular customers only. There was also a black market which was illegal, and often involved those who may have already been on the wrong side of the law. It is perhaps fair to add that a certain amount of minor bartering and 'fiddling' was tolerated, but profiteering and black marketing were considered worse than the despised queue jumping!

The first food items to be rationed were bacon or ham (4oz per person per week), butter (4oz) and sugar (12oz). Everyone was issued with a ration book and their quota of rationed food had to be purchased from where the ration book holder was registered eg. the local grocer and/or butcher. If rationed items were sold to a customer who was not registered with a particular retailer, this was in breach of the regulations and from time to time such cases were reported in the press. One such example involved the unauthorised sale of meat from a travelling shop owned by the Silverdale Co-op. This resulted in both the firm and the driver being fined (*Staffordshire Advertiser* 14th December 1944). Additional ration books were also issued to pregnant women, children under five years old, and those of school age.

Women in particular spent hours queuing for both the rationed and un-rationed items such as fresh fruit and vegetables. For some, such occasions were an irritating inconvenience, but generally on the village from what I recall, they were in a way a social happening, giving an opportunity to hear the latest news or gossip. In any event, I personally did not regard shopping with my mother as a chore. I was always fascinated by such distractions as the dart cash and carry machines - the contraptions which conveyed cash and receipts overhead from one part of the shop to another. The Silverdale Co-op also had another type of cash and carry device at its Newcastle Emporium which worked with an ingenious system of pneumatic pipe-work. This conveyed your money in a canister, and any paperwork, to the cashiers in the bowels of the store. Moments later, this would return with any change and a receipt. Although anticipated, it never ceased to make me jump as it was ejected into a wire basket with a mighty thunk! I enjoyed the experience of shopping with my mother and meeting people and perhaps more importantly, learning to appreciate the value of money. Mum was our home's Chancellor - a financial wizard and administrator who made a little go a long way.

Bananas were unavailable for most of the war, and whilst I can remember experiencing my first taste, I can only assume that it was after the war. On the other hand, oranges were reserved for children and arrival of consignments was often announced in the press. For example, the *Staffordshire Advertiser* on 25th March 1944 informed readers of the arrival of 2,000 cases in Stoke, this being the first instalment of a total allocation of 6,800 for the area. Each case contained 200-300 and the press report indicated that ration book holders were entitled to 1lb each. From time to time, the arrival of other consignments would be announced by the media such as Sicilian lemons and Portuguese sardines (*Staffordshire Chronicle* 4th March 1944), brought in by the indomitable unsung men of the Allied merchant fleets.

We children also received priority milk allowances. Distributed daily to pupils at school in small bottles with a cardboard top, these could often be frozen solid on arrival at the premises in winter. However, in our case, Mr Bromley the caretaker would place thc crates by central heating pipes to thaw. In addition, children also received free cod liver oil and concentrated orange juice, both of which were dispensed at the clinic at Crown Street/Vale Pleasant. We seemed to be habitual visitors to such premises with our mothers where we received regular weigh-ins and also were given inoculations by the nurses. We were also allowed 4 eggs on our ration books to every egg per adult. However, the fresh egg supply was sparse, but once introduced, dried egg powder became a useful alternative.

Throughout the war, more types of food became rationed. On 8th February 1943 tinned fruit came under the 'points' system. This allowed customers to purchase goods, usually luxury items, in addition to the basic ration. It allowed some choice, but restricted the number of tins anyone could purchase. However, the rationing system itself had built-in flexibility, allowing the alteration of amounts etc., depending on availability. Other foods such as bread, fish, offal, sausages and fruit were 'off the ration' but often in short supply resulting in long queues at times as word spread of a fresh consignment.

Fortunately, as far as North Staffordshire was concerned, there was one item of fare which was not rationed and could provide a reasonably priced substantial snack. This was the oatcake! Generally perhaps seen today as weekend fare, they could nevertheless be eaten at any time, providing you could find an oatcake shop which opened on weekdays. According to historian Fred Hughes, the history of the delicacy goes almost back to Medieval times, originating in the Moorlands of Derbyshire as a thick cake. When adopted by the working class of North Staffordshire, it was watered down so that it went further, and fillings such as bacon and cheese were added. In the late Victorian period, oatcake shops were springing up all over the area. Silverdale was fortunate in having two in the 1940s, Plants on Crown Street and Harrisons on High Street. At an early age I queued with my mother in Plants' corner shop and watched in admiration as the batter was skilfully poured over the hotplate and then, a few moments later, seeing the resultant oatcakes placed on the counter. We could not then get home fast enough to sink our teeth into the delicacy!

Those fortunate enough to have a garden or allotment embraced the Government's 'Dig for Victory' campaign which eventually ranged from humble plot to ancestral acres. Even the Tower of London moat was drained and used as an allotment! It meant home grown produce was to hand and it remained throughout the war the mainstay of many family meals, helping out an increasingly restricted diet. Even those without a garden were given advice on how to nurture a crop of mushrooms in a box in a dark corner! But on the allotments, holders not only exchanged tips on growing methods, fertilisers, and seeding times but also recipes for chutneys, jams and preserves. Information could also be given to novices about storage of certain summer crops for the winter months. Allotments helped to bond communities and the older gardeners often said that when you had worked hard to grow food, it

Harry Barnett enjoying a break at his allotment on the Acre, Silverdale. *(Harry Barnett).*

Bumper crops on the Park Road (Back Lane) allotments, Silverdale. *(Marjorie Horton).*

The Foresters Arms (or 'Corner Pin') photographed by thc late Harry Corfield shortly before demolition in the early 1960s. *(Hadgett Collection).*

Harry Plant outside his oatcake shop at Crown Street/Victoria Street in the company of Bill Lavin, the village road sweeper. (Photograph by the late Jack Deakin).

The Acre allotments at Silverdale, originally laid out in the 18th Century. *(The Sentinel).*

A train leaving Silverdale station.
The spire of St. Luke's Parish church may be seen in the background.

tasted that much better, and was unlikely to be wasted.

On occasion, my father would also return from the mine with a rabbit which had been caught or shot in the fields surrounding the colliery complex. Reminiscent of a magician's trick, this would be revealed from the large poacher's type pocket inside my father's work coat and then skinned and stewed in a large brown pot. How my father came to acquire the carcass I cannot recall. He was certainly not involved in any poaching activity, and I can only assume that the rabbits were obtained from a workmate, some of whom were 'dog gun men', particularly those from the outlying villages of Crackley Gates and Halmerend. Rabbits could be purchased from butchers and made an excellent meal, being reminiscent of chicken, and the skins could be sold on!

I assume that I, like other wartime children, did not take kindly to sweet-rationing. However, donations from parents and relatives helped to find ways around the system. Alternatively, certain sweets such as 'Victory V' lozenges and herbal tablets were un-rationed, and sometimes we were reduced to purchasing these. Another important source of confectionary was American servicemen. Most were exceedingly generous and, after all, we were the most shameless scroungers! Based at nearby Keele Hall, the Yanks were often seen on the village. They would on occasion be seen sitting on the wall of the Bethel Chapel at the corner of Chapel Street and Church Street and few could resist our eager faces and appeals of 'got any gum, chum?' Often, packets of gum, chocolates or sweets, and even money, were handed over making us believe that Christmas had arrived early! The Americans frequented Spooner's Dance Hall in High Street and their confident swagger was a great attraction to some of the girls. Mary Statham (now Mrs Clews) also recalls seeing them walking in small groups in Cemetery Lane where they would patronize the Forester's Arms (or Corner Pin pub) which abutted Rosemary Buildings where she lived. They might have been seen behaving amorously with the girls at the Jollies fields or in the area of Job's Wood off Back Lane.

The introduction of food rationing, later extended to clothing, was well managed from the beginning coming under the helm of Lord Frederick Woolton. Much of the system's success was due to his insistence on thorough planning, fairness and good presentation. Having developed a knack of getting his message across in a friendly manner, he became a popular, respected wartime Minister. His name lives on, being associated with 'Woolton Pie'- a simple vegetable dish which became a symbol of British wartime cooking, the recipe for which may still be found in certain cookery books today. Woolton also lent his support to a BBC radio programme called 'The Kitchen Front'. Broadcast daily after the 8am news, it attracted some 14 million listeners with contributors such as Marguerite Patten providing recipes and useful household hints. Another popular contributor was the Radio Doctor - Dr Charles Hill whom I fondly remember. Listening on our radio to his earthly comments, robustly delivered, certainly helped to influence me and no doubt many other children as we finished breakfast and prepared for school. Examples of the good doctor's wise words included hygiene, brushing teeth after meals, 'be regular', and eat your greens, an excellent source of vitamins. Dr Hill even recommended dandelion leaves which my maternal grandfather enjoyed regularly in season, on a sandwich. No one could afford to be a fussy eater but there certainly were some unusual ones such as nettle soup, stewed dandelions, beetroot jam, cabbage soup etc. Watercress also grew in abundance in a lovely, clear stream which ran down the fields off Back Lane between Meadow Cottages and the allotments. A useful addition to salads in season, some also used the aquatic plant for soups.

Some families were fortunate in receiving food parcels from abroad. In our case, we had an occasional parcel from relations from my mother's side of the family - the Lloyds of Cheadle who had emigrated to New Zealand. The parcels included such items as tinned fruit or meat, but also the most delicious fruit cake - I particularly remember this!

As happens today, people attempt to avoid rules and regulations. The period during World War II was no exception! Illegal ways to supplement the food rations were often found. For example, animals had to be registered in order to supply them with food and also for their slaughter. It was difficult sometimes for officials to check the number of piglets in a litter - they could not be everywhere. On the other hand, it was relatively easy to pass one piglet on, unnoticed, for fattening on waste from the kitchen. Pigs were sometimes hidden in sheds and isolated buildings and left to grow very fat, the more the better!

With all the advice from nutritionists on food which was available, rationed or otherwise, helping to ensure that the population was well fed, it is hardly surprising the claim is often made that we were all healthier then than today, even with the benefit of modern science. Apart from perhaps mild complaining about coupons and rationing, there was an overall attitude of good humour. The need to pull together and get on with it blossomed. 'We're all in this together' was the general attitude, and it was that which helped bring us through those difficult times.

Nine
Any more fares please?

In my childhood, Silverdale was well served by public transport, both road and rail, and I've often heard it claimed that it was easier to travel then by such means to various parts of North Staffordshire than it is now. In any event, car ownership was uncommon and therefore public transport was vital.

Villagers had the choice of three omnibus operators and hence three respective timetables. The Potteries Motor Traction Company (PMT) was the main service provider for the conurbation, its routes connecting the village with Newcastle-under-Lyme, Burslem, etc. Travelling to Halmerend and Audley was achieved by Poole's Coaches which regularly ran thorough Silverdale, but using High Street only. Journeys into Newcastle using this service travelled via Knutton. As part of the public service, newspapers from Morrall's Newsagents on High Street, and prescriptions from the local pharmacy were conveyed to Halmerend and the outlying area by Pooles.

The other independent operator, and possibly the most popular, was Duggins Princess Bus Service. They used Dennis vehicles, later replaced by Sentinel coaches. One Dennis coach was small with wooden slatted seats and was locally known as 'the Matchbox!' Owned by Tom Duggins and based at Priory Garage, Newcastle, his coaches only operated on a regular direct route between the village via Silverdale Road into Newcastle and return. Villagers today love to reminisce about the service and some of the tales of the 'Princess' and its crews are legendary!

Tom Duggins employed two crews of driver and conductor. 'Little' Edgar Dean and Ernie Peake would work one shift, and Jim Turner and Eric Mothershaw the other. On occasion, Jim's wife was employed as 'stand-in' conductress. Statutory regulations appeared to mean little or nothing to Duggin's crews - the numbers of passengers carried at peak times were unbelievable! Commuters could be standing, packed like sardines, from front to rear! The passenger loading was achieved on account of the crews, at times, seemingly 'disregarding' the official timetable as they sped through the village picking up passengers ahead of the timetabled PMT service. *'Put that child on the luggage rack'* or *'Open the rear door'* I've heard quipped as Ernie Peake wrestled down the aisle collecting fares. But it was pleasant travelling on the buses. Passengers generally knew each other, manners were better than today and it was a social event. On arrival in Newcastle at the Guildhall terminus, the passengers would quickly disembark, whilst conductors would temporarily retire to the Globe Café opposite, to replenish the crew's tea canteens.

Ernie Peake in his 'civvies'. *(Claude Hadgett).*

The atmosphere on buses was completely different then, with coaches often packed to the limits and many of the passengers smoking. They would also talk to each other as opposed to many commuters today sitting in their own little world listening to music through earphones. Some conductors were renowned for 'entertaining' commuters as they performed heroics getting through the crush collecting fares. Men and schoolchildren were expected to give up their seats to women and elderly passengers, and most followed this practice. On Duggins' buses at school times, children would be 'encouraged' to sit three on a seat, or stand in favour of their elders.

Duggins' crews, like those of other operators, hand punched tickets at this period, producing little coloured circular pieces of paper. These were recycled as wedding confetti. Many married couples on the village can lay claim to having been showered with Duggins' confetti on their wedding day! The cost of fares was normally a few pence which could result in the conductor's bag soon becoming heavy with coinage, particularly at peak times.[1] On some buses, if a passenger did happen to tender a ten shilling note, he would likely be given a fistful of coins in change as a warning to produce the correct fare on the next journey! Also only the conductor was permitted to operate the bell!

My recollection is that omnibus services were very reliable, with perhaps the exception of adverse weather conditions. Even so, there would have had to have been a considerable amount of snowfall before transport was disrupted or services curtailed. Extreme foggy conditions also resulted in cancellations, the situation not being helped then by excessive amounts of smoke emanating from the pottery kilns and other local industries. On such occasions I, as a child, have walked with my parents from the village to my maternal grandparent's home at Etruria, a distance of 4 miles. The lack of public transport did not prevent visits to relations!

At Etruria, I was able to closely observe another important form of transport. The Trent & Mersey canal ran behind my maternal grandparent's house in Salem Street. Immediately opposite the end of the garden was the Anderton & Mersey Weaver Company Wharf. This was always a hive of activity and could be observed over the wall by standing on a box. Barges seemed to be continuously passing, some pulled by horses, and many destined for the nearby Wedgwood factory. Others would have been transporting ware from there for export, but some of the narrow boats were also passing through the area to and from Cheshire.

Silverdale was also well provided with an excellent passenger and goods rail service. Rendered by the London, Midland & Scottish Company (LMS), the branch lines and other assets had been taken over from the former North Staffs Railway (or The Knotty) two decades earlier. Regular trains ran in an easterly direction into Newcastle-under-Lyme and Stoke-on-Trent to connect with London trains etc., whilst to the west Pipe Gate, Norton in Hales and Market Drayton could be accessed at times for race meetings, etc. After hostilities ceased, special trains also used this picturesque route for excursions to Ternhill aerodrome for the air shows.

Being wartime, troop movements and the transport of vital goods took precedence over civilian travel plans and, at times, trains could be delayed or services cancelled. Also, with the necessity for armaments, special workers' trains ran daily from the village to the Royal Ordnance Factory at Swynnerton, the coaching stock being parked overnight in the tunnel just outside Silverdale station.[2] In its heyday, an average of 8,000 travelled daily to the factory from various parts of North Staffordshire. The Cold Meece branch, as it was known, was a 'ghost line' veiled in wartime secrecy, never appearing in any public timetable.[3] A further workers' train ran to a new halt called 'Wedgwood' at Barlaston, built to serve the famous pottery company's modern factory which transferred from Etruria in 1940. In addition to the goods and passenger services, coal from Kents Lane Colliery was conveyed by rail into Brampton Sidings or Pool Dam Sidings at Newcastle-under-Lyme.

The village railway station was a fascinating place. There were engine numbers to collect, and trains of one type or another seemed to be arriving or departing frequently. Not only this, but I had an opportunity to view the trains working close at hand, including the busy shunting engines of the colliery. Being next to the giants with their hissing steam and wheels clanking, and witnessing the firemen throwing coal onto a roaring fire before unleashing the monster - it was, and remains, another world! Normally, the clicking of signal wire and a distant piercing whistle preceded the arrival of a locomotive before it rounded the seemingly tight bend at the rear of The Brighton cottages. Belching smoke, fumes and ashes would then envelope station staff and intending passengers as the train came into the station. Standing on the platform, the whole of the structure seemed to shake beneath your feet before the monster groaned and hissed to a clanking halt.

At the end of one of the platforms a water tower was situated, with an extending canvas pipe. At times, crews of steam engines would replenish their water supply at this point and, to us children, this in itself was an amazing operation to watch. One of the crew would draw up the pipe and insert it into a hole on the top of the locomotive's tender and then suddenly it appeared to come to life as water rushed through it from the tank and into the engine. On completion of the task, the pipe would be dropped over the side from the locomotive. However, prior to returning to its former limp hanging position, anyone standing close, like we used to do, would be likely to receive a shower from the surplus water as the pipe wrestled to a halt!

Just outside the station was a signal box which not only controlled the various rail movements and branch line connections in the area, but also the level crossing from Station Road into the Kents Lane colliery complex. Through the large windows of the box, the bank of burnished levers could be seen which, on being operated, caused a piece of line elsewhere to form another junction. If the windows were open, bell signals could be heard as they were received from other boxes down the line. Operated by a large wheel, reminiscent of that on the bridge of a ship, the level crossing gates would be closed on the approach of a train. This was closely monitored by the children as they loved to steal a ride on them, until admonished by the railway staff!

For those who had an urgent need, or were fortunate to be in a position to afford to use it, the village possessed a taxi service during the 1930s/1940s era. Operated by Peter Cotterill, his garage was situated in Chapel Street, adjacent to the Silverdale Aerated Mineral Company (or Pop Works). At other times, he could be found working with his wife at their successful confectionary business in Church Street.

Notwithstanding the fact that the village was well served by public transport, it should not be overlooked that members of the public were more inclined to walk at this time, some no doubt for economic reasons, but others for pleasure. Whilst Silverdale had a good selection of retailers, some residents would nevertheless walk the two miles or so into Newcastle, and return with their shopping using the bus service. Others, would walk into the town daily to their place of work. An example is the window cleaning Whittle family who walked into Newcastle pushing a wooden trolley containing their ladders. They would often be seen early in the morning walking along Silverdale Road. However, if the weather was inclement, Mrs Whittle and daughter might journey into town on the bus, leaving Mr Whittle to walk with the trolley. At this time not as many mothers went out to work, so prams were pushed to the shops. There was a completely different attitude to life. Few of us would perhaps volunteer to be taken back to those times, but is it not any wonder that the claim is often made that the population in general was healthier, and even happier then?

Notes

1) It was not until 1951 that PMT succeeded in an application to the Traffic Commissioners to raise the minimum fare from one old penny to one and a half pennies.
2) C.R. Lester. *The Stoke to Market Drayton Line* (The Oakwood Press) p48.
3) Rex Christiansen & R. W. Miller. *North Staffordshire Railway* (David & Charles) p260.

Silverdale signal box and level crossing with the station in the background. *(Basil Jeuda).*

The junction of Station Road and Sneyd Terrace. One of the railway station staff is shown returning from delivering goods by hand-cart. *(Brian Nixon).*

Ernie Peake, the clown prince of Duggin's 'Princess' Bus Service, pictured with one of the company's Sentinel coaches. *(Alan Scott).*

ROF Swynnerton employees arriving at Cold Meece station during wartime. Silverdale station was the starting point for this 'secret' service. *(Basil Jeuda).*

The former Primitive Methodist Chapel (the 'Prims') in High Street, Silverdale.

Silverdale Prize Band photographed at an area competition. *(John Johnson).*

A Salvation Army Band leading an anniversary procession in Church Street, Silverdale. Photograph by the late Jack Deakin.

Ten
I can hear music

Music has always been a fundamental part of North Staffordshire's history and culture, the area having been long associated with prize winning choirs and choral societies. It was certainly not unusual to be a member of both. At Silverdale I was acquainted with a number who were in a chapel or church choir but who also joined the famed Ceramic City Choir of Stoke-on-Trent following its formation in 1942.

This was a period when the war news in Britain was possibly at its blackest, with a constant recital of defeats and deprivation. Some 270 choristers took part in a performance of Handel's 'Messiah' under Dr Malcolm Sargent (later Sir) at the Victoria Hall, Hanley after which he suggested that the choir should be made permanent. Always keen to promote new choral societies, he was then also engaged in a personal wartime drive to secure work for musicians. He agreed to become the conductor, then controlling the generation of employment, and the Ceramic City Choir became another of his great successes.[1] Sargent had a reputation for inspiring amateur singers and there is no doubt that his appointment as permanent conductor had a number of advantages. He was very popular with audiences, particularly the ladies, and his connections ensured the attendance of first class artistes at Ceramic City Choir concerts and over the next few years, wartime or not, local audiences were treated to some of the finest available.

Many choristers attended rehearsals immediately following work, travelling some distance, making use of public transport. Some experienced difficulty due to discontinuance of services after normal working factory hours and, if necessary, would walk to the rehearsal rooms. On the mornings following a big event, such as a performance of a major oratorio, 'inquests' would be held amongst the passengers commuting to work on the buses, and if top female artistes such as Gladys Ripley, Joan Hammond or Kathleen Ferrier had been in attendance, fashions would be a topic of conversation amongst female passengers.

Many of the area's fine choirs have resulted from a legacy of mining and Methodism. No one put it better than Philip Broadbent, conductor of the nearby Audley Male Voice Choir when he observed that *'Methodism and mining make a strong cocktail.'* There was also a view that the area's choirs benefited from the influx of the Welsh and that this was *'a winning mixture.'* This was certainly the belief of the late Bob Davies, one time conductor of the Newcastle Male Voice

Choir. Bob was a very popular resident on the village, and a physiotherapist. Having experienced a few scrapes in my time and having had to visit his consulting rooms in High Street, I can testify to his expertise! Some local choirs, including the Silverdale Male Voice Choir, certainly won a number of competitions in Wales, beating the Welsh at their own game! A coach load of supporters usually accompanied the choir to the Welsh competition venues and if they were winners, they would sing the test piece on Crown Bank on their return. I witnessed such an event on more than one occasion in my childhood.

On Silverdale, Methodism was represented by four chapels with large congregations and choirs and there was strong, but friendly rivalry between them - the Bethel in Church Street; the United Methodist Free Church in High Street; The Wesleyan in Newcastle Street; and the Zion Primitive (or 'The Prims') in High Street. In my family, life centred around the latter. Other places of worship on the village were the Parish Church of St. Luke in Church Street; the Pentecostal in Cross Street; the Elim Pentecostal in Albert Street; the Congregational in Victoria Street; the Bethel Temple in May Street; the Salvation Army Citadel in Vale Pleasant and the Roman Catholic Church in High Street.

Being baptised at 'The Prims' I regularly attended the Sunday School which was then under the supervision of the long serving Superintendent, Joe Mothershaw. The highlight of the year, dependent on your point of view, was the celebration of the Chapel Anniversary in May (or 'Charity' as the event was known locally). This was the occasion when the children appeared on stage in chapel in their new outfits. For the boys, perhaps not unexpectedly, this was not such a popular experience - having to wear new clothes, and also a prior requirement to rehearse on sunny weekday evenings instead of playing in the open air. Rehearsals and the final performance were under the charge of Doris Thornhill. A lovely lady with the patience of Job, she performed miracles and motivated the children until they seemingly achieved perfection on the day.

Whichever denomination, anniversary day was a long one, particularly for the very young. In the morning all would assemble at their own church or chapel and then parade around the streets of the village accompanied by a brass band, stopping at various locations en route to sing a hymn whilst donations were collected from the residents, many of whom would come to the door and join in the singing. On return to the chapel, they were usually treated to buns and soft drinks. In the afternoon and in the evening, the children would again return to the building and appear on a portable stage which had been hurriedly erected a few days earlier. Here, they would, hopefully, give a first class performance in their

The Prims' long-serving Sunday School Superintendent, the late Joe Mothershaw seen 'in action' during the chapel anniversary procession. (from *Life on the Dale* by Barry Williams).

A chapel anniversary procession in Abbey Street, Silverdale. *(Barry Williams).*

Kathleen Ferrier, who first performed Brahms' Alto Rhapsody at Silverdale in 1943. *(Kath Hopcroft).*

Harry V. Keat MBE seen centre with glasses with members of the Etruscan Choral Society. He was CEMA organiser for North Staffordshire and introduced Kathleen Ferrier to the area. *(Kath Hopcroft).*

new clothes, proudly watched by parents and relatives and the premises would be packed with extra seats being provided in the aisles. On that day most preachers would appreciate the occasion in not giving too long a sermon from the pulpit, otherwise some of the very young children were likely to fall asleep and have to be removed from the staging. Sad to say, it is doubtful if the portable stage would be allowed in the present health and safety climate. Towards the end of the service an eagerly awaited announcement would be made of the amount of money raised, everyone hoping that it would have increased from that of the previous year, whilst coincidentally being a larger sum than rival chapels. The event then traditionally closed with the singing of John Ellerton's hymn 'The day thou gavest, Lord, is ended' which we on stage were always pleased to hear! Of course, it should not be overlooked that these events were popular for the local clothing retailers as the 'charity season' was a very busy time of year for them.

At an early age I became accustomed to the annual performances on the village of oratorios such as Handel's Messiah and Judas Maccabaeus, Mendelssohn's Elijah, Stainer's Crucifixion, whether sung in my chapel or at another place of worship. At 'The Prims' the building would be filled to capacity for such events and if you had a preference for seating, then early attendance was essential. It was certainly not unusual for some families to be seated an hour or so before the evening session commenced, and during this period the organist would give a recital. It was certainly a long evening for him at the console! In my childhood and the years beyond Clifford Shenton and Gordon Holdcroft were extremely popular organists at 'The Prims' and they introduced me to other music and composers. In particular, Gordon Holdcroft himself arranged some orchestral music for the organ, one of my favourites being Finlandia by Sibelius. On opening his session with this, Gordon certainly pulled all the stops out!

Special concerts were also held in some of the village chapels even during wartime. Featuring celebratory soloists, some went on to become legendary figures. For example, Kathleen Ferrier gave her first ever public performance of Brahm's Alto Rhapsody Opus 53 at 'The Prims' in 1943 with the Etruscan Male Voice Choir. This was a work which was eventually to bring her fame and a recording award. On that evening, prior to the concert, Kathleen was heard practising her scales in the vestry after which chapel steward Frank Seabridge predicted 'that girl will go far!'[2] At this period, Kathleen was building up her repertoire, trying out numerous items in public for the first time in the area. Singing in the North Staffordshire area always gave her 'great pleasure.' Her concerts were always well attended and she found the audiences appreciative.[3]

The residents of nearby Crewe were also fortunate to be the first to hear Kathleen sing 'Che Faro' (What is life?) from Gluck's *Orfeo and Eurydice* in a recital on 10th March 1943 accompanied by the great Gerald Moore.[4] She went on, of course, to make the aria her very own but in the meantime she gave many wartime morale boosting concerts in the Potteries area, some in factories. In these, it was not unusual for her to appear in the dual capacity of contralto soloist and pianist.

There was much talent on the village at this period having been trained or assisted in no small way by a number of highly respected local music teachers including the likes of Cressie Hough and Arnold Johnson. It may have been a war period, but it was not a cultural desert!

Notes

1) See *Trentham at War* (Churnet Valley Books) by same author. Chapter 7.
2) Ex. information Mrs N. Woodvine who was present at the concert.
3) *The life of Kathleen Ferrier* (Hamish Hamilton) by Winifred Ferrier. p56
4) Ibid p52.

Vale Pleasant, Silverdale looking in the direction of the Five Road Ends. The Salvation Army Citadel is on the right of the photograph (from *Life on the Dale* by Barry Williams).

Eleven
Theatre, cinema and the fun of the fair

One important area for keeping spirits up during the dark days of the war was entertainment. Having said that, as soon as war was declared, all public places of entertainment such as theatres, concert halls and cinemas were initially closed down to avoid the possibility of people being killed in crowded places during a bombing raid. However, after a short period and no immediate threat of the anticipated raids, many venues re-opened but with air raid precautions in place. Also, in London and some major cities, it was not unusual for a theatre to be taken over by the forces' entertainment unit ENSA.

I recall being taken to the Theatre Royal, Hanley as a child, particularly during the pantomime season. Then the show ran for eight weeks and the venue would be packed out nightly. In defiance of Hitler, a note in the theatre programmes warned patrons that in the event of an air raid warning the show would go on - *'However, anyone wishing to leave the theatre at this point should walk - don't run!'* Wreathed in fag smoke, as places of entertainment then were, with perhaps the smell of wet raincoats, the theatre shows were nevertheless magical occasions. In an age before television, the price of a ticket brought patrons into the presence of some of the biggest stars of the day. The cheapest seats, providing you didn't suffer from vertigo, were in the Gods, being squashed high up under the ornate ceiling. Surveying the stage from this area of the theatre was like looking down the face of the Eiger!

The Royal was possibly at its peak in the 1940s, but naturally as a child I did not appreciate the importance of the place with its vast auditorium and gilded balconies, designed by the renowned theatre architect Frank Matcham. Then variety drew the audiences and stars such as Albert Modley, Norman Evans, George Formby, Nat 'Rubberneck' Jackley, Betty Driver, Charlie Chester and Rob Wilton appeared and boosted morale at a time when it was needed. Another favourite was Old Mother Riley, although at the time I did not realise that she was, in fact, a man - the actor and comedian Arthur Lucan! The theme of the act was that Old Mother Riley was always trying to stop her attractive and headstrong daughter Kitty (actually Arthur's wife!) from being seduced and taken from her. She threatened to 'marmalise' any man having designs on Kitty!

My own personal favourites were the musical comedy acts which appeared from time to time in the variety shows. I loved the crazy antics of Dr Crock & his Crackpots and Sid Millward & his Nitwits, having revelled in the recordings of Spike Jones from childhood. I have to confess, however, that as I grew older, I much preferred the local pantomimes which were staged on the village by the chapels, youth clubs etc. There was so much talent on Silverdale and despite the performances being only accompanied by a piano instead of a full theatre orchestra, these shows were produced very professionally, were most enjoyable, and generally sold out.

Nevertheless, I loved the Royal and, as time went on, supported it on a regular basis until like many other similar venues, it closed as a theatre and went over to bingo in 1961. The only gripe I had as a child regarding the Royal was that, on occasion, the show would run late. As a result, my parents and other patrons would be 'clock watching' and sometimes had to leave early to ensure that we caught the last bus returning to the village. This meant that we could miss part of the final act which was, in any event, disappointing as it usually featured the star - the prime reason for purchasing a ticket in the first place!

Cinema also proved to be a most important form of public entertainment during the war. Many of the Hollywood movies such as *Gone with the Wind* drew huge audiences. On the village the Roxy in High Street kept residents and those from outlying areas entertained, its programme changing three times a week, and running a children's show on Saturdays. The content of this performance could actually determine the way boys walked down the street on leaving the cinema. If we had seen Tom Mix, William Boyd or Buck Jones, then a leisurely 'western' cowboy walk with one's pals might be adopted. Alternatively, if a war film featuring enemy Nazi forces had been on the screen then a high stepping march, John Cleese style, might be in order. Attendance at the Roxy's weekly Saturday children's 'club' or 'tuppenny rush' was an essential for village children. Perhaps not offering the varied entertainment as the Newcastle or Hanley cinemas with their children's talent shows, quizzes etc., the Roxy performances were nevertheless very popular. They offered films suitable for the younger audience including cartoons and serials such as a western or Flash Gordon, the episode of which generally ended on a cliffhanger. If the film broke down, there would be a near riot with the children stamping their feet and shouting which sometimes had to be brought under control by the staff. But, generally, the village children were well behaved. A visit to the Roxy on a Saturday was a highlight of the week.

I also enjoyed an occasional visit to the Regent in Hanley because of the additional entertainment from Felton Rapley at the mighty Wurlitzer which rose out of the floor as he was playing his signature tune. Then having finished his performance, he returned slowly, mechanically, with the illuminated instrument into the orchestra pit, waving as he went. By the standards of the day, the Regent was a futuristic piece of design and the venue attracted patrons like a magnet. Seating over two thousand, queuing to obtain admission for a performance of a popular film was certainly not unusual, and the line could stretch a lengthy distance in both directions along the street and around the corner! Most cinemas, the Regent and Roxy included, featured a newsreel which included reports on the progress of the war. To us children the period was an exciting one, strange as it may seem. But we were shielded from the conflict to a certain extent by parents and didn't fully appreciate what was going on. Having said that some daily newspapers provided wall maps to enable events and progress to be plotted. Some boys became veritable plane spotting experts gathering information from cigarette cards they had collected, even identifying aircraft from the sound of engines!

Visits to Hanley were particularly remembered with affection when Pat Collins and his fun fair arrived for two weeks at the beginning of August. This was the combined period of potters' and local mineworkers' holidays. When the camp had been set up in Regent Road, it was wonderful to wander around the site and soak up the atmosphere and the smells of the throbbing steam engines and candyfloss. There was every type of entertainment from the waltzers, dodgems, chairoplanes, ghost train, test your strength ('hit the bell') and sideshows to coconut shies, hoopla and roll a penny. In those pre-television days, Pat Collins was a welcome visitor during the local holidays and thousands gained much pleasure from his arrival. Others merely wandered around the fairground even if they couldn't afford to actually participate in the activities. In fact, for some, attending the wakes was their annual holiday!

The arrival of the circus in the area was also very welcome. Chipperfields, Fossetts, Bertram Mills and Billy Smart all brought their shows to the fairground at Hanley, and also to Brampton Fields at Newcastle. Elephants and stars from the shows were a familiar sight, parading through the streets announcing their arrival. They attracted hundreds of spectators as they made their way to Hanley from Stoke station. I was often taken to see the event and like other children loved the occasions when you could see the large animals close up. Elephants, lions, horses, and even bears were popular acts - cruelty was never an issue then. At the site the public could also wander around the animal quarters and see them being fed. Some circus tents were massive, cathedral like in size. Chipperfields alone was said to hold six thousand! The performances to me were magic with the band virtually playing non-stop throughout except when there was a dramatic silence as a high wire or trapeze act reached a 'death defying' climax. I was also spellbound by some of the large and unusual items of transport that the companies used to convey their equipment. When Billy Smart arrived after the war, his fleet appeared to consist of mighty ex WD vehicles. It is also worth mentioning that when the circus was in town, locals could sometimes find temporary employment, assisting on site in tasks such as erecting the big top, or dismantling it at the end of the visit.

For me, however, a visit to Hanley was never complete without a visit to my Aunt Annie's shop at the bottom of John Street. One of my most favourite relations, Aunt Annie was a colourful character with a great sense of humour. Her shop, whilst not strictly being of the 'open all hours' variety, hardly ever seemed to close. Even when it did, neighbours would rattle the front door latch to request a loaf etc and she would never refuse them. My aunt also had a coal business in the rear yard. This was a wonderful place to play, weighing coal on the huge industrial scales - and making myself unpopular with my parents by dirtying my best clothes when we were about to attend the theatre!

When reminiscing on the subject of entertainment at this juncture, one cannot possibly dismiss the workingmen's clubs. They were well supported in membership on the village, whole families with children attending. On certain nights, entertainment would be provided by visiting artistes. In the 1940s, Silverdale had two WMCs, that in Newcastle Street being known as 'Bottom Club' and the Chapel Street/Five Road Ends premises being referred to as the 'Top Club.' On one occasion, my Uncle Herbert Taylor was present at a magician's performance at the Top Club when he won a five shillings bet. Affectionately known as 'Beaut', Uncle Herbert was a wonderful character with a glass eye. The magician, like everyone in the audience, knew Uncle Herbert well, but commenced to annoy him by asking after each successful trick - 'How about that, Beaut?' Eventually, Uncle Herbert leapt on stage and challenged the magician by betting him five bob that there was one trick that he could not perform. The performer accepted, whereupon Uncle Herbert whipped out his glass eye saying *'How about that, mate?'*

Other venues of entertainment, as far as I was concerned, were certain village shops. Whetnell's fish & chip shop was a clearing house for gossip and news but it could suddenly descend into whispers when children were present. In later life, I am reminded of the occasions by comedians Les Dawson and Roy Barraclough in their hilarious portrayals of Ada and Cissie. A normal conversation along the lines of 'she's had an operation for...' would suddenly break off to require lip reading to complete the sentence! This, of course, was how female operatives in the local mills maintained conversations against the noise of the machinery. I also loved to sit in Jack Deakin's barbers shop, particularly when miners were present. Jack himself was a card who was a member of a local concert party, performing as a comedian and magician, but when miners were also in attendance at his Church Street premises, the banter was like a 'Command Performance' to me. In the excitement, should anyone have attempted to reach the door without paying, Jack would shout 'Don't forget your change!' A bus stop was located a few yards from the front door of the shop and Jack's son Michael recalled that, on occasion, someone would step through the door and shout 'what time is the next bus due?' Not one to miss an opportunity, the response would be 'sit in the chair, you'll be done in time to catch it!' In later life I came to appreciate these 'performances' when famous comedians on being interviewed, claimed that they obtained most of their material by listening to the public in the street or on public transport.

For most families in North Staffordshire in the 1940s, holiday destinations were North Wales or Blackpool, assuming that they could afford a break at all. In our case, Mrs Thomas's guesthouse in the backstreets of Rhyl was a regular venue, including wartime. Our journey by rail would normally commence at Silverdale station with changes at Stoke and Crewe. Being the combined miners' and potters' holidays, extra trains would be in place. At Crewe in particular, I had to be kept on a 'tight rein' as I had been known to wander on occasion, wishing to explore the huge station complex. On arrival at Rhyl, a small army of children with barrows or prams were present and they would transport luggage to your hotel or guesthouse for a few pence. They either walked with you, or went on ahead. In any event, Mrs Thomas's premises were close to the station and we never made use of taxis.

I thought Rhyl at that time was wonderful. In the company of our parents, my cousin Ann and I would play on the beach, splash around in the rock pools, sunbathed, eat ice cream and went to the fun fair. Personally, I was never happy with donkey rides. The animals always looked so sad, giving me the impression that they really didn't want to be in that form of employment at all. On one occasion, one donkey relieved itself over my aunt's dress! Ann and I wondered if the animal was taking some form of revenge.

I loved to hire a bicycle and ride it in an enclosure on the promenade. As I did not possess a bike of my own at the time, I regarded it as a real treat. Sometimes there was also an opportunity to visit the circus which appeared at the resort's Pavilion Theatre. We took advantage of public transport to visit the countryside, visiting such venues as the Marble Church at St. Asaph. There was always something to do at the seaside in those far off days and the weather fine and sunny.

The Workingmen's Club (Top Club) at the Five Road Ends - the scene of Uncle Herbert's extraordinary performance! Photograph by the late Harry Corfield. *(Hadgett Collection).*

Bella Whetnell proprietor of the Church Street fish & chip shop. *(Claude Hadgett).*

NEXT WEEK ONCE NIGHTLY AT 7.0
Matinees Thurs. and Sat. at 2.30

Sadler's Wells Opera Co.
AND ORCHESTRA

HERE FOR A SEASON
Commencing May 25th
ROY LIMBERT'S
MALVERN CO.
In a SEASON OF PLAYS

Cast will include

Peggy Burt	**Maitland Moss**
Phillipa Gill	**Arthur Mainzer**
Faith Noble	**Robert Del Kyrke**
Phyllis Rietty	**Robert Rietty**

The Plays Produced by
SYDNEY BLAND
WITH THE CONNIVANCE OF ROY LIMBERT

Trains to Hanley on the Loop Line—Congleton, etc., 4.33; Newchapel, etc., 5.20; Kidsgrove, etc., 7.27; Blythe Bridge, etc., 5.15; Cresswell, etc., 7.15 p.m.

From Hanley to Blythe Bridge, etc., 8.10; Cresswell, etc., 10.25; Congleton, etc., 9.0; Kidsgrove, etc., 10.50 p.m. (10.30 Sats.)

KEATES LTD., PRINTERS, PARKER ST., HANLEY.

THEATRE · ROYAL
HANLEY

"THE POTTERIES OWN"

Proprietors : THE POTTERIES THEATRES LTD.

LICENSEE ARTHUR BIRKETT — GENERAL MANAGER PERCY E. HUGHES

Telephone · Stoke-on-Trent 5251

BOX OFFICE OPEN ... 11-0 A.M. TO 8-30 P.M.

MONDAY, MAY 11th | TWICE NIGHTLY | 6.0 & 8.0

Return Visit of The Famous Success

"SMILIN' THROUGH"

By ALLAN LANGDON MARTIN

WITH

WILLIAM RODERICK ERIC WETHERELL

THEATRE NOTES

In the Event of AIR RAID WARNING being received during a performance you will be notified from the Stage, and the Show will go on.

If you leave the Theatre, WALK—DON'T RUN to the Exit you have chosen.

* The Management reserve the right to alter advertised programmes if necessary.

PROGRAMME **2D.**

SWINNERTON'S
MILK BAR
PICCADILLY HANLEY.
OPEN UNTIL 8 P.M. DAILY.
T. T. (Tuberculin Tested) MILK

FORSTER'S for FRUIT
A Firm with a Record of 35 Year's Standing
T. FORSTER & SONS
MARKET HALL
HANLEY
WED. — FRI. — SAT.
Choice Fruits at Lowest Market Prices
FRUIT — for — HEALTH

Telephones :
2361—2362—5003

GRAND HOTEL.

(Messrs Trust Houses Ltd.)

*

Luncheons, a la carte, or table d'hote 2/6

Snack Bar.

Parking,
Free during Meals

ENGLISH AND CONTINENTAL CATERING unsurpassed

WINE CELLARS
to meet the choice of the most fastidious

Musical Interlude by the Theatre Royal Orchestra under the direction of Reg. Lawton

PROGRAMME

CAST (in order of their appearance)

John Carteret ... ... ERIC WETHERELL
Dr. Owen Harding WILLIAM RODERICK
Ellen ... ... IRIS FRASER-FOSS
Kathleen Dungannon PHYLLIS BAKER
Willie Ainley ... ... MICHAEL BLYTHE
Kenneth Wayne KENNETH RAYMOND
Mary Clare ... CONSTANCE CHAPMAN
Rose ... ... PEGGY RAMSAY
Sarah ... ... ROSEMARY GUNNER
William ... ... JOHN MERCER
Edward ... ... MICHAEL BLYTHE
Jeremiah Wayne KENNETH RAYMOND
Moonyeen Clare ... BETTY ENGLAND

The Play produced by William Mollinson

SYNOPSIS OF SCENERY

Act 1. The Carteret Gardens, 1914
Act 2. The same. Fifty years before
Act 3. The same. 1919

Stage Setting designed and executed by W. J. Hemsley and constructed by P. Calvert.
Ladies' Costumes created for the production by Mayfair.
Shoes by Gamba, London.
Men's Clothes by B. J. Simmons & Co., Ltd., London.
Wigs by Gustave, London.
Cigarettes by Abdulla.

The Song "Smilin' Through" will be sung during the action of the Play by Peggy Ramsay, late of the Carl Rosa Opera Co.

Manager ... ... Eric Wetherell
Stage Director ... ... T. C. Leybourne
Stage Manager ... ... Rosemary Gunner
Master Carpenter ... ... F. Darnton
Wardrobe Mistress ... ... Nina Gerrard
(For Thornwall Productions Ltd.)

WHY NOT HAVE A JOULE'S STONE ALE

Tyres Batteries
NORMEIR
Phone 4128
BEST POSSIBLE SERVICE
HANLEY
STOKE
NEWCASTLE
USE OUR
CAR PARK
Marsh Street
Nearest to this Theatre)

FOR
RADIO & PIANOS
BY ALL THE MOST FAMOUS MANUFACTURERS.
Deferred Payments Arranged.
J. C. Sherwin & Son
MARKET SQUARE HANLEY.
Est. 1855.

The author on holiday at Rhyl with his parents during World War II. *(Ann Barnes).*

Just ignore the photographer, we want to get to the beach! - on holiday with cousin Ann and our respective mothers at Rhyl. *(Ann Barnes).*

Jack Deakin's barber shop, the scene of many a comedy performance.

The late Jack Deakin - a cut about the rest - a self portrait, in his barber shop in Church Street.

Twelve
Sit up straight!

Some may regard the prospect of being raised in a mining village as 'the pits', but having been born at Silverdale - I loved it! The presence of two good schools on the village helped to ensure that pupils were given a good start in life and some of us made friends for life. In my case, schooldays were spent at Silverdale County Primary School, affectionately known on the village as 'The Board School' Being towards the end of World War II when my schooldays commenced, the infants' premises on Mill Street remained an ARP & Nursing Station. As a result, the department was temporarily housed in alternative accommodation in the Juniors (or big school) on the opposite side of the road.

My mother used to walk me to school initially, and other families would join us on the short route. However, given that traffic was not as busy as it is today, I was soon entrusted to make the journey on my own, as were fellow pupils. What I didn't comprehend at the time was that school was compulsory, and not somewhere to go when you have nothing else to do! One afternoon when I hadn't returned home at the normal hour, my worried mother hurried to the school only to learn that I hadn't attended. Retracing her steps, she found me happily playing with other children in a communal air raid shelter in Victoria Street. Whether my playmates had intentionally played truant I'll never know, but after an explanation and belting from my father (a blacksmith's striker with a heavy hand!) I soon appreciated that school attendance was not an option. I was also put in fear of the School Board man!

The seat of learning comprised two typical Victorian single-storey buildings with lofty ceilings and large high level windows. Originally, boys and girls would have entered the big school via separate entrances, clearly labelled as such, but by the time my schooldays commenced, this was no longer the case. The classrooms were spacious, light and airy - cool in Summer, warm in Winter. The latter was entirely due to the devoted efforts of the popular caretaker, Mr Bromley, who lived in premises adjoining the infants' school. He ensured that the central heating was in working order, and at no time can I recall the school being closed due to malfunction of the system - or wintry conditions! Both infants' and juniors' buildings had multifunctional halls, that in the juniors' being the larger. This had a stage, and the room was used variously for morning assembly, dining purposes, physical training, concerts, road safety demonstrations by the local constabulary, and as an examination centre when the 11 plus season was in session. Outside each building was a large play area with toilet blocks. In the warmer weather physical training would perhaps be performed outside in the yard, whereas supervised cricket, football and other seasonal sporting activities were conducted on the nearby Jollies fields, or on playing fields off Park Road (Back Lane).

Playtime at school was an essential part of the day. Designed to provide pupils with exercise and fresh air, it also helped to encourage social skills and teamwork. Unlike today, playtime was not supervised by any adult! We played the usual games of conkers, marbles, and hopscotch plus football and cricket, but also joined the girls at times with skipping ropes. When this occurred, there might be 'skipping chants' especially if a group was participating, this involving children rushing in and out of the ropes as their birthday month might be called. Double Dutch skipping was also played which was more difficult, with skippers and turners using two ropes together. Although simple pleasures, the games taught us valuable lessons about friendship, fun and fairness. During playtime, I recall the playground alive with noise and excitement.

During my attendance at the school, teaching staff of the Infants Department included Miss Shaw, Miss Ellams and Miss Hinchco, the Juniors' staff comprised Miss Balance, Miss Brown, Mr Whalley ('Choca'), Mr Wellings, and Mr Faulkner ('Daddy'). In particular, I recall that Miss Hinchco ruled us pupils with the lift of an eyebrow! If needed, however, she could also deliver a most accurate rap across the knuckles with a ruler for such offences as talking in class. Today, this well loved and respected teacher would possibly be faced with a charge of assault, but at the time it was normal practice, being part of the discipline training. We were also being continually 'encouraged' to sit up straight at the desk, and not sprawl across it!

For a brief period of my village schooldays, the headmaster was Frederick Hugh Cork (1878-1970). A Daleian himself, he commenced his career as a pupil teacher at the school at the age of 14 years. Having then survived the Somme in World War I, he qualified on demobilisation at Crewe Training College and returned to the school, eventually attaining the post of headmaster. This he held until he retired at the age of 65. A lifetime spent in one school must qualify as a record, and Mr Cork was highly respected on the village. A firm believer in adult education, he also provided special evening classes for the miners, teaching them maths, English language and English Literature.

Fred Cork was a hard act to follow and this fell to Charles Holland (1905-2003) who, following his appointment in 1946, soon stamped his own individual authority and style on the school. He proved to be an energetic and enthusiastic man, a good disciplinarian, strict, but kind and patient. Frequently impressing upon us that he expected nothing but the best, in the years to come he went on to guide and inspire his pupils, large numbers of whom went on to universities and successful careers. As one former pupil put it - *'his teaching provided the skeleton keys to the world beyond the classroom, the home and the village.'*

Basically, we were taught not only knowledge, but the meaning of courtesy and imagination. In addition, we were taught a sensible degree of discipline and respect, not only for those who taught us, but in all walks of life. Contrary to opinion in some quarters, this did not harm us in any way, nor stunted our growth, but rather provided a firm foundation on which to build a youngster's behaviour and attitude to life and society as a whole. In addition, village teachers developed in me a natural flair for reading and writing which was also encouraged at home by my mother.

From time to time school visits were organised to local tileries and other industries, to help pupils gain an appreciation not only of their importance to the local economy, but also of working conditions and, in the case of some, prospects for future employment. Visits were also made to the school by a number of speakers who gave talks on the mining industry, etc. Other regular visitors included the 'Nit Nurse' and school dentist, whose equipment was enough to discourage attendance at dental clinics for life!

In complete contrast, pupils were escorted on nature rambles in The Acre where teachers would point out the wildlife. We also on occasions undertook excursions by coach to Snowdonia and the North Wales coast. From these, I'm confident that we gained as much pleasure as pupils today experience from trips to Europe. In addition we visited Dudley Zoo where we met children who had not seen farm animals before. Their answer to the question - where does milk come from was likely to have been bottles! However, with the close proximity of farms to Silverdale, I and my fellow pupils certainly knew what cows were and where milk came from. We also, from time to time, saw sheep and cattle being delivered to the village railway station where they would be placed in pens until ready to be driven through the streets to nearby farms or abattoirs.

A self-confessed lover of music, Mr Holland formed a school choir and under his personal attention it soon won acclaim from adjudicators when

Victoria Street, Silverdale - the scene of my 'truancy'! Photographed by the late Harry Corfield in 1957 *(Newcastle-under-Lyme Reference Library).*

The former Silverdale County Primary Juniors' Building (or Board School to villagers). *(Alan Scott).*

Silverdale County Primary Infants' Building which was requisitioned during World War II as an ARP & Nursing Station. The premises are now used as a social centre. *(Alan Scott).*

The class of 1950. Form IV, Silverdale C. P. School with headmaster Charles Holland to the left and teacher Keith Faulkner to the right. The author is in the rear rank, fourth from the left.

appearing at local festivals. The choir not only gave concerts on the village and at churches in the district, but also travelled regularly to Buerton Chapel which was a popular venue. To us children, this was a marvellous day out with refreshments provided in a local farmhouse. Certain pupils, including myself, were also fortunate in being chosen to represent the school in the massed choirs at the Newcastle Youth Festival. These annual concerts, held in the Municipal Hall, and under the baton of Dr Percy Young, were splendid occasions.

Perhaps my favourite teacher at Silverdale was Mr Faulkner who had responsibility for Form IV which comprised the eldest pupils at the school. He had a keen sense of humour, a good teaching style and the skill of making everything appear interesting. He also introduced us to a number of books, including Captain Marryat's *Children of the New Forest*, which have remained firm favourites. The local library staff also visited the school at regular intervals with a supply of books from which we made our choice. This encouraged us to become avid readers and prepared us for later on when we could visit the village library, then situated opposite the Globe pub, in our own right. Being presented with your own library card was like being 'presented with the keys of the kingdom' as one teacher observed. But I remember all the teachers as being kind, dedicated and competent, and consider my period at the village school a most happy one.

In 1950 I was successful in gaining a place at Wolstanton County Grammar School, having taken the 11 plus examination. Credit for this must also go to Mr Holland who personally ensured that all those taking the exam were fully prepared and up to standard, introducing homework for candidates. To us from the village, Wolstanton was a completely different world where boys addressed each other only by their surnames and teachers wore black academic gowns in class. But that, as they say, is another story.

Thirteen
Christmas on the Dale

To us children, the approach to Christmas was naturally an exciting period. Before the actual festival of the nativity, there were parties at the school and concerts to which parents were invited. Also, at chapel, there was a pantomime and Sunday School party. The Board School party, in particular, was greatly supported by parents who, despite rationing, always conjured up 'goodies', some items no doubt especially hoarded for the occasion. In art class, tasks included the design and creation of Christmas cards for parents, and calendars for the coming year. Paper chains made by the pupils decorated the classrooms, together with locally collected holly. Guided by teachers, letters were composed to Father Christmas politely requesting presents we particularly desired. The times being what they were, and parents' economic situation were important factors as to whether we were successful!

Visits were made with parents to the large departmental stores in Newcastle, Stoke or Hanley to see Santa. Strange as it may seem, this was not a particularly popular event for me as I did not like entering the darkness of Santa's grotto - Claustrophobia perhaps? I did, however, love to visit the toy departments and see the latest Dinky toys. Like many other youngsters, I hoped that on Christmas morning there might be an impressive boxed Dinky gift set, but at an early age I learned what I might realistically receive. Other 'wants' usually included a Hornby train set which could also include models of railway workers, station staff, passengers and farm animals. Hornby certainly captured the imagination of boys at this period. Today, the toys are collectors' items, recalling a host of memories from a less complicated era. Dinky toys are also regarded today as a manufactured history of transport, and a brilliant example of model maker's art. Also on my wish list was a Meccano construction kit with its interchangeable parts. Jigsaws, plasticine, and games such as Ludo and Snakes & Ladders, together with books, were also popular presents.

As I grew older, I appreciated receiving a comic annual such as the Beano. Originally published in 1938, this weekly publication became an icon and having the annual was a must! My favourite characters were Lord Snooty, Pansy Potter and Jimmy & his Magic Patch. Less affluent days meant that only one comic was allowed weekly, but that is not to say that other comics were a closed shop, as there was an elaborate system of barter in place. Thus, having worn the print off whatever publications you had, you generally acquired standing arrangements with your pals to exchange yours for theirs. Children then were perhaps more natural wheeler-dealers than today with a keener sense of values. For example, if one comic cost more than another, or had more pages, then you could negotiate two for one.

Being employed at the colliery, my father's close colleagues included skilled craftsmen including joiners, blacksmiths etc, and in my younger days it was not unusual to receive a present which had been made exclusively for me. Toys of this category which I particularly recall with fondness include a scale model of the liner Queen Mary, and a bren gun which operated with repetitive loud noises, reminiscent of the genuine article - my parents no doubt wishing that I had received a more 'peaceable' toy!

The excitement of waking on Christmas morning to experience the weight of presents lying at the foot of the bed, and hearing the rustle of paper is something I am unlikely to forget. Santa never let me down! At this time it took longer to open presents - one learned to be patient! There was no sellotape or special gift paper, nor instant ripping apart of parcels as children are inclined to do today. Presents were wrapped in paper and string, which were carefully undone and, like more or less everything else, retained for recycling. However, I generally found that it was worth the delay to discover the exciting contents.

There was also the possibility of the late arrival of a present by post, as there were deliveries on Christmas Day. Some friends and relatives believed in posting greetings cards late, particularly those intended for local delivery, so as to ensure arrival on the special day. If the word 'local' was endorsed on the envelope, the card would be delivered within 24hrs, despite the amount of mail. The postmen on the village were respected and regarded as friends at any time, but particularly during the festive season, always being greeted warmly in the streets.They were often whistling as they went about their daily tasks, regardless of the war situation. Those delivering newspapers also appeared to have a similar disposition, and these jobs were always sought after. Newsagents had no need of advertising for newspaper boys, there was usually a waiting list for vacancies!

In our family, Christmas morning was essentially a visiting period, and we were certainly not alone in this respect on the dale. Temporarily leaving my mother to prepare the 'special' lunch, Dad and I would call on relations and friends on the village to wish them the compliments of the season, and generally a drink of port or sherry and mince pie would be offered on such occasion. Children would be offered a glass of lemonade, whilst taking the opportunity to inspect the presents that other youngsters may have been left by Santa on his round. I was always intrigued by those presents which my cousin, Arthur Brereton had received. He, being interested in DIY, was more likely to receive a junior carpenter's kit and it was not unusual, by the time of our arrival at his home, to witness something under construction.

Meanwhile at home, my mother in turn would be greeting visitors, whilst at the same time, juggling pots and pans over a hot stove as she attempted to prepare lunch. Today, this is referred to as multi-tasking! Visiting was undertaken on foot, as none of the family then had vehicles. So despite having consumed food and drink, after covering a reasonable mileage since breakfast, we were always ready for lunch!

On Christmas morning it was not unusual to hear the sound of carols in the streets, particularly from the area of the Five Road Ends. Sometimes, this would be accompanied by a band or at least a small group of brass instrumentalists. The singers would be members of a local choir or augmented from the village chapels and church. The music was always appreciated, and served to remind residents of what the celebrations were all about.

We certainly did not have to 'dream of a white Christmas', to quote Irving Berlin's famous song - it was there! I particularly remember the festive season of 1944 as in common with many other parts of the country, North Staffordshire received heavy falls of snow. The *Sentinel* described the local scene as *'a mantle of glistening white on trees, hedges, bushes, and roof tops, giving a pleasantly seasonal touch.'*[1] As a result, many travellers found themselves stranded during the Christmas break as no public transport services were available. Conditions were so severe, that even those who did have vehicles chose not to drive. Among those stranded were Canadian servicemen from HMS Fledgling at Mill Meece. Having 'taken the liberty boat' to Newcastle-under-Lyme, they were unable to return to the base. Fortunately, provision was made for their temporary accommodation in the town, and naval officials advised of their predicament. Otherwise they would, of course, been regarded as AWOL (absent without leave). Other service personnel returning to the base at Mill Meece in Royal Navy transport had to abandon vehicles and complete the journey on foot![2]

Attending school presented no problems at such times as it was conveniently situated on the village and a short distance from home.

Daleians' nearest main shopping centre - an aerial picture of Newcastle-under-Lyme taken in the 1940s. *(The late Ewart Wildon).*

A view taken in Ironmarket, Newcastle in the 1940s, showing one of the large departmental stores. *(The late Ewart Wildon).*

Nevertheless, in the winter, it was not unusual for the snow to be of a depth which was over the tops of wellingtons. Taking advantage of the situation, the occasional snowball fight would ensue to and from school. At no time during such weather conditions can I recall either of the village schools being closed. The popular school caretaker Mr Bromley always ensured that adequate fuel stocks were available and that the heating apparatus was in full working order.

I would help my father clear the paths to the front and rear of the house, and also those of neighbours who were perhaps elderly and unable to undertake the task. Ashes from the bins would be spread to prevent slippage. In the event of the few drivers having difficulty in the wintry conditions, help would be given to extracating vehicles from the deep snow. It really was a question of helping one another until conditions improved, particularly the more vulnerable. One accepted this as normal, and as a child, I grew up to respect this.

Notes

1) *The Sentinel* 27th December 1944
2) Graham Bebbington *The Fledglings* (Churnet Valley) pp 72/73.

Church Street, Silverdale in wintry conditions - photograph by the late Jack Deakin.
All the buildings shown on the left no longer survive.

Fourteen
The Circle of Life
- hatches, matches & dispatches

During World War II, many young men and women took a gamble on parenthood and official records reveal that over 4.5 million babies were born during the six years of hostilities. Servicemen suddenly granted leave before embarkation faced the real possibility that it may be the last time that they would be together. Some women then decided to take the risk of bringing a child into the world at such time because they wanted to have something 'to hang on to' in the event that their husbands did not return. As a consequence, in the grimness of 1942, after years of decline, the nation's birth rate began to climb. The situation locally is confirmed by data supplied by the Office for National Statistics. Whilst separate figures are not available for Silverdale, there were 1,060 births recorded in the catchment area of the former Borough of Newcastle-under-Lyme in 1941. In 1942, the number of births rose to 1,155. In the neighbouring City of Stoke-on-Trent there was a similar situation with 4,459 births recorded in 1941, and 4,844 in 1942.

As part of the government's recognition of the vital importance of maintaining the nation's health on the Home Front, emergency maternity homes were set up in some areas using requisitioned properties. In addition, pregnant women were given high priority in evacuation from areas likely to be under attack. Even so, like many of my friends and relations who were conceived at this time, I was born at home. Given that the majority of families on the village did not have the benefit of telephones and cars at the time, I gain the impression that doctors and/or midwives did, nevertheless, manage to be present in time for arrivals. But it was also not unusual for alternative arrangements to be made for an 'unofficial' midwife residing nearby to assist on those odd occasions when the professionals were unable to be present. Such persons could possibly have been a former nurse or merely someone who had learned by experience over a period of time. These members of the community would be regarded as responsible and trustworthy, having built up a reputation.

Whilst obviously not remembering the event, I understand that Dr Percy George Johnson was present at my birth. This information was revealed to me by my mother in later years, I apparently having given her a difficult time on my entrance. I believe that I arrived at what may be regarded as a reasonable hour, unlike my lifetime friend Mary Statham (now Mrs Clews) who decided to claim a ladies' prerogative and arrive late at around midnight! This caused her father to make an early attempt at the 4 minute mile, hastening up the village from the family home at Rosemary Buildings on a foggy, winter night, to call out the doctor from his home. Thankfully, all went well.

Possibly the best known midwife/district nurse on the village in my childhood was Mrs Clare Mullineux. Out of respect, she was always addressed or referred to as Nurse Mullineux! Her daughter Christine recalls that her mother was often called out at all hours from the family home in Church Street. A very smart, pleasant, homely lady, she was often seen 'on duty' wearing her uniform with pride and carrying her black Gladstone style bag. Having arrived on foot to assist in a birth, the order was then given - *'men and children out of the room and put the kettle on!'* Unlike today, it just wasn't a mere male's place to be present at a birth, although they generally could be trusted to open the door for the midwife and to put the kettle on. Incidentally, the hot water was not for making tea, but essential for keeping everything clean and sterilised.

Our GP, Dr Johnson, was small in stature and always immaculately dressed. As a child I often wondered how he managed to drive his large saloon car, as he always appeared to have difficulty in seeing over the steering wheel and through the windscreen! A highly respected practitioner, he resided in a bungalow in Mill Street with the surgery and waiting room forming an extension to the rear. No appointments system was in place at this time, the doctor seeing patients on a first come, first served basis. On occasion this could result in a lengthy delay in receiving a consultation, particularly if medicine was required, as the doctor also dispensed this at the surgery. Similarly, a long wait might ensue if the doctor received a call to respond to an emergency situation. Like some of my school chums, I did not like Dr Johnson because he was inclined to do 'nasty things' to me such as inserting needles into parts of my anatomy. Even worse, he sent me to hospital! But, of course, in later years I came to appreciate what a fine doctor he was and how well he had served the community.

During the war the status of babies and their mothers rose dramatically, again part of the government's strategy for maintaining the nation's health. Extra milk, free concentrated orange juice and cod liver oil were available via the ration book, and maternity care for mothers and infants came free or at a nominal charge. The result was that the country produced healthier babies than before, despite the stresses of family separation, anxiety and the situation generally. However, being wartime, there was a positive lack of certain goods on the domestic market front including babies' necessities. Prams, pushchairs and clothes were hard or impossible to obtain and mothers had to borrow, exchange or simply make do. As it happened, both my parents came from large families. Consequently, there was no problem, as such items were simply handed down, including toys. I distinctly remember my father taking delivery of a Mickey Mouse tricycle one day for me, and it wasn't even Christmas! This was later exchanged for a larger tricycle, until I eventually progressed to two wheels.

I can't particularly recall having attended any weddings during the war period, but they did occur in the family as did others on the village. Nevertheless, I can remember attending matrimonial events in the post war period in the 1940s when rationing remained in force. Again, it was a question of make-do with families combining to save coupons to obtain items of clothing, or altering a bridal dress which was a treasured heirloom. Parachute silk was a much sought after material for recycling into bridal wear and this could sometimes be obtained if you knew the right person. Alterations would involve the skills of local dressmakers/seamstresses to produce a 'new creation.' There were a number of these accomplished ladies on the village at the time, but our family always tended to use Mrs Dolly Whittaker in May Street for any alterations to clothing. There were generally no clothing problems for members of the armed forces when tying the knot as both men and women tended to marry in uniform.

Wedding breakfasts, if affordable, were likely to be held in Sunday school premises, pubs or workingmen's clubs. I attended a number at the rooms situated above the Co-operative shops in Victoria Street. Arrived at via a long winding staircase, this was spacious accommodation with a kitchen for preparation of food, and a large room with a stage and piano. There never appeared to be a shortage of food for such events, but in later years I was to appreciate that this was a result of clever meticulous planning with friends and relatives having hoarded certain items or saved coupons to ensure that there was a good, impressive spread for the special day. Entertainment was always provided after the meal, and most venues had a piano. If no pianist was available, a musician would be hired for a small fee. Personally, I remember piano accordionist Jackie Mayer accompanying dancing at some functions. Also, if there were any singers present, and most families had choir members in their ranks, there would be songs or duets of the time.

A 'Bonny Babies' competition held at The Villas, Silverdale in 1942 in aid of SSAFA funds. *(Brian Nixon).*

Over a period of time there appears to have grown a tradition on the village of married women 'retaining' their maiden names! I noticed this in my schooldays and in some quarters it remains to this day. For example, my cousin's spouse is referred to as 'Nora Beech - Arthur Brereton's wife!' This quaint custom seems to have been going on since at least the early 20th century, but at least one knows precisely whom you are talking about. I've often quipped that Silverdale is a place where no-one gets married, which raises a few eyebrows amongst strangers!

In my childhood, on those unfortunate occasions when a death occurred in a family, there tended to be certain 'customs' which were adhered to before the attendance of an undertaker to remove the body from the house. In most families there was what might be termed an experienced 'layer-out'. Upon being called, he or she would assist in making the corpse 'presentable', even shaving the deceased if required. On learning of a bereavement neighbours, relatives and friends living in nearby streets, would draw their curtains as a mark of respect. Also, children would be told not to play or make any noise in the vicinity of the deceased's house. A similar instruction would also apply in the event of a neighbour being sick or on shift work and this formed part and parcel of everyday life on the village. Woe betide any child who disobeyed!

Being a mining village, funerals tended to follow a similar pattern, whether the deceased had mining connections or not, and it was considered that everything had to be seen to be done correctly. On the day of the funeral, the deceased would lie in the front room of the house with the coffin lid open to enable those who wished to pay their last respects. At the appropriate time, the coffin was then placed in a hearse for the journey to the chapel or church, the vehicle moving off slowly with the procession of mourners walking behind. On occasion, if the family could afford, a saloon car might also be supplied by the undertakers to convey females or elderly relatives. One of my own earliest memories is of walking behind the hearse at the funeral of my paternal grandfather. Brook Street, where my grandparents lived, was lined with residents and the men removed their caps as the cortege passed. Sadly today, in this hi-speed technological world, a funeral cortege barely receives a second glance.

Following the funeral service and committal, it was the custom for mourners to return to the deceased's house for light refreshments. If the accommodation was not sufficiently large enough, normally the front room or parlour, then that of a neighbour might also be used. In this case, trestles and tables would be hired, or loaned without charge, from a chapel or workingmen's club. My parents offered the opportunity for use of our front room to neighbours for funeral refreshments and as a child I assisted in the transport of seating etc. I can remember such occasions clearly, merely one example of the tightly knit community. Families ensured that a good quality gravestone was provided which, at that time, would have been an appreciable amount. Miners could be lavish at funerals, but poor in life. They remain a proud people.

Clare Mullineux (nee Evans) newly qualified as a SRN. *(Christine Ward).*

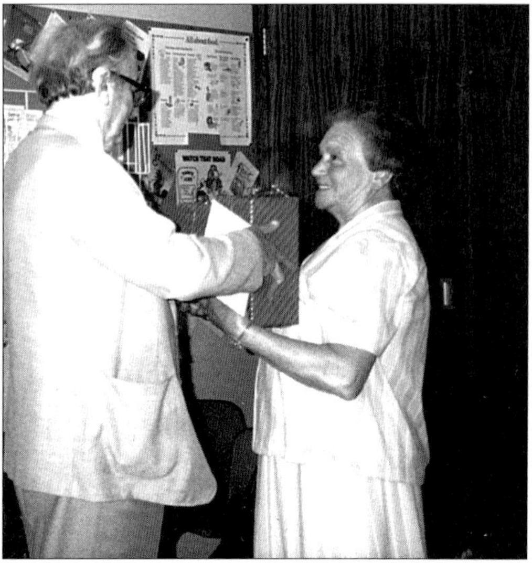

Dr Ron Jolly makes a presentation to Nurse Clare Mullineux on her retirement in 1972. *(Christine Ward).*

Playtime at Rosemary Buildings with Greg Deakin (rear), Ralph Humphries, Mary Statham & Graham Humphries (centre) and baby Anthony Williams in front. *(Mary Clews).*

Fifteen
VALCO's

Like most people, I came to appreciate the taste of ice cream at an early age. Later in life, I contemplated the likely number of mining villages which would have been fortunate to possess an ice cream parlour. I can't imagine that many had an establishment like Valco's. I also found that because of the relationship between Italians and the ice cream industry, there is a tendency to think that it is an invention of the Victorian period, but it is much older, its history complex.

Suffice to say that the history of ice cream has been an evolution, from drinks cooled with ice and snow to semi-frozen lemonades; from water ice to dairy ice cream; from ice cellars and snow pits to the heat extracting effect of adding salt to water and thence to refrigerator technology based on ammonia gas. Today, we can't imagine ice cream without refrigerators or freezers, but ice was consumed when they did not exist! For example, the Greeks and Romans mixed drinks with snow. Furthermore, the Persians drank sherbets, a sort of sugar water cooled with ice or snow, commonly mixed with rhubarb. As time went by, many of the landed gentry had ice houses or ice cellars at their stately homes, the Sneyds at Keele Hall a local example. But with the advance in the 19th Century of ammonia operated freezing machines, blocks of ice could be produced artificially with the result that production was no longer dependent upon the availability of natural ice during the winter months. This helped to accelerate the spread of ice cream throughout the western world.

Victorian Britain's ice cream industry was largely run by Italians, part of the tide of economic migrants who came over in the 19th Century, the majority from Northern Italy. Until the advent of the edible cone around 1888, ice cream was either taken home wrapped in wax paper, or licked out of a small glass known as 'a penny lick' which was then supposedly wiped clean and re-used. However, this practise was eventually made illegal on health grounds in 1926.

In the 20th Century, another wave of Italians came in, predominantly from the south and Sicily. Many passed through London and the 'Little Italy' colony in Clerkenwell, going on to establish communities in various parts of the country, some eventually coming to Staffordshire. Among these was Goffredo Valco who initially came to Burslem, then Chester, before settling in Silverdale in 1904. He appears to have been the earliest to establish himself in the area.

Born in Rapallo in 1879, the locals apparently could not get their tongues around 'Goffredo' and he became known as Alf! (Daleians have a way with words!). Although the village eventually had one or two more ice cream men, according to his son George, Alf was the only one to manufacture his own 'true' product. The first Valco ice cream parlour was situated on the corner of Crown Street/Victoria Street (later Plant's oatcake shop). In the meantime, he married Maud, a girl from Onneley, and together they had seven children. Subsequently, the ice cream business relocated to 3 Crown Street where my generation fondly remember it.

The Valco family lived at the property which was understood to have been a former pub. The interior certainly gave that impression, having retained its furniture including lounge type seating around the walls and heavy tables with wrought iron legs. All Alf's ice cream, sarsaparilla and soda drinks were made on the premises. Whilst being very popular with young people, the ice cream parlour was also frequented by certain characters who liked to chance their luck on Mr Valco's one armed bandit machines which were discreetly hidden. In addition, for the amusement of patrons, a ring board and shooting gallery were located at the rear of the premises. I was also to learn in later years that cigarettes were sold from 'under the counter' in packets or loose. Alf's business was not confined to the village. Ice cream was sold in the Madeley and Keele areas using a horse and cart. The horse, named Billy, was also regularly used to collect ice from Clewlows opposite the Smithfield in Newcastle.

With the coming of World War II, Parliament passed the Emergency Powers (Defence) Bill which included new laws placing restrictions on almost every aspect of life. Amongst the legislation was a measure providing for the internment of anyone who might have been considered a threat to the interests of public safety or the defence of the realm. This resulted in a number of fellow ice cream manufacturers such as the Sidoli family of Newcastle and Mario Togneni of Hanford being detained for a period as 'aliens.' Similar well respected people of foreign extraction were detained across Britain, a large number being from well established business families whose loyalties were entirely with this country. Some were interned locally at Prees Heath, whilst others were sent to the Isle of Man. The measure was very unpopular with the indigenous population and caused riots in some areas. One person who appreciated the situation was the local Member of Parliament for Newcastle - Josiah Wedgwood IV (later Lord Wedgwood) - and, having supported Jewish refugees fleeing from Nazi Germany, he also fought for those who found themselves detained under the new emergency laws. As for the Valco family, they were not detained. In any event, Alf himself had become naturalised some years earlier, and his three sons were then serving in the North Staffordshire Regiment (Royal Artillery), and anyway Alf had served with distinction in the British army as a despatch rider - not the easiest of jobs - in the Great War of 1914-1918,

After World War II and its food rationing, sweets continued to be rationed, but ice-cream was not, so the British tended to eat far more of this. Sadly, Alf Valco died in 1954 and the business on Crown Street closed. Not only that, his recipes were never divulged and they died with him. It was the end of an era. However, in my mind's eye I can still see him standing behind the counter wearing his trade mark trilby and cream coloured overall.

Goffredo Valco (otherwise Alf!) *(Author's collection).*

Goffredo Valco with daughter Agnes, shown outside the family ice cream parlour, Crown Street, Silverdale c.1905. *(Author's collection).*

Sixteen
Victory - at a price?

Servicemen and women reading news of the victory in the war in Europe, May 1945. *(The Sentinel)*

In May 1945 the war in Europe came to an end with the signing of Germany's unconditional surrender by Field Marshal Keitel. 'Victory in Europe' otherwise VE Day, saw a great explosion of excitement and celebration. London was the focus of the biggest festivities, but Newcastle-under-Lyme's celebrations included a Victory Parade through the town and a thanksgiving service at St. Giles Parish Church. According to the Sentinel the church was packed and the service was relayed by tannoy to the crowds in Red Lion Square.[1] Some can also recall the spontaneous dancing of the 'hokey cokey' and the conga in the town's Ironmarket.

For the more culturally inclined, special thanksgiving concerts were held in the Victoria Hall, Hanley one being given by the Stoke-on-Trent Choral Society. Out at Mill Meece, celebrations took on a somewhat different perspective at the Duke of York public house. Surprisingly, fighting broke out between Canadians from nearby HMS Fledgling and locally based American troops. Apparently, the fracas resulted from a difference of opinion as to 'who had contributed most to win the war!' Peace was only restored after the landlord telephoned the naval base for assistance.

Yet for all the good news, there was still more suffering as the extent of Nazi evil was unravelled by way of press photographs and newsreel footage showing the liberation of the Auschwitz, Belsen and Buchenwald concentration camps. Those of us of a certain age retain crystal clear mental pictures of the scenes shown at the local Roxy cinema. Perhaps only then did we begin to fully appreciate what the war was about. Some families who had relatives in the forces who were involved in the actual relief of the camps are aware that they never fully recovered from witnessing the men, women and children in ragged striped pyjama type prison outfits caged behind barbed wire, and the stench of the piles of naked emaciated corpses.

The final end to the war was not to come for another three months with the surrender of Japan, and this only materialised following the nuclear bombing by American aircraft of Hiroshima and Nagasaki. On 15th August, following days of negotiation, Emperor Hirohito broadcast to his people that the war was over. News of the Japanese surrender was formally broadcast in Britain by Premier Clement Atlee and 'Victory over Japan' (or VJ Day) saw another upsurge of joy and celebrating. Church bells rang out over the countryside at intervals during the day and street parties were much in evidence, together with celebratory dances at all the usual venues. The local media reported that whereas the streets of Stafford were *'not as gaily decorated'* as for VE Day, *'nevertheless crowds turned out in spite of drenching rain throughout the day.'*[2] At HMS Fledgling, Mill Meece a huge bonfire was organised crowned by an effigy of Emperor Hirohito which made 'a wonderful blaze.'[3]

It seems that my former schoolmates and I have few memories of actual events on the village following the announcement of the Japanese surrender. As young children we could not have really appreciated what it was all about. After all, during our short lifetime, war had been the norm. Records show that 15th and 16th August were declared public holidays in which the nation celebrated and offered prayers of thanksgiving. Some of us can remember parading around the village waving flags, after which we dispersed into the Bethel Chapel Sunday School. Here we were treated to sandwiches, jellies and cakes which resourceful mothers had somehow laid on. Buntings were much in evidence in streets and shop windows, and my parents and neighbours displayed Union Jack flags from the bedroom windows.

As demobilisation proceeded, millions of servicemen began to return to civvy street and attempt to return to normal life. These included a number from our family who I had only seen in uniform for brief periods when they were on leave, among them two of my mother's brothers. One, having been in Germany at the time of surrender, returned with what I regarded as 'treasure trove' including a large Nazi flag emblazoned with the swastika, and a collection of enemy regimental badges. His older brother returned from the Italian campaign passionately describing a performance of Verdi's *Aida* which he had seen when stationed in Verona. Like many others, he did not talk about the actual fighting, nor his service with the Royal Engineers at all.

An Aunt had served with the Women's Land Army in Norfolk and thoroughly enjoyed doing 'her bit'. I never understood why she returned to work in the pot-banks having heard the stories about her time on the land. Some servicemen had been away for so long, perhaps as prisoners of war, that a child may have wondered who the soldier was walking up the garden path! In other households, the position about loved ones may have been unclear by reason of them having been reported as 'missing' so there was no celebration there. At school we were aware of the tragic situation that one or two fellow pupils found themselves in where no father would be returning.

Whilst the surrender of the Japanese revived the scenes and emotions of VE Day, their sheer inhumanity towards allied prisoners of war and civilian internees then became apparent and their rescue became the most urgent task of the liberating forces. There were over two hundred POW camps, including the notorious Changi jail where thousands had already died of starvation, disease and brutal treatment. Other prisoners were forced to work as slave labourers on the infamous Thai-Burma railway (later known as the 'Railway of Death' and featured in the film 'Bridge over the River Kwai'). The project involved laying a railway track of 250 miles or so through some of the most inhospitable and toughest terrain imaginable. It was said that every sleeper laid represented a lost life. The construction was a multinational effort that was to become synonymous with sadistic cruelty, death and disease as well as heroism, valour and true comradeship in the face of adversity. No doubt like many others, I have never understood how the Japanese expected the workers to maintain such a harsh and unrelenting construction schedule in the face of starvation and diseases such as malaria. As one former POW commented - *'had they provided us with proper food and medical treatment, the project would have been completed sooner.'* The Japanese had a habit of bayoneting captives and it was cruelties such as these that eventually resulted in a number of their leaders and officers being tried for war crimes. Some returning POWs spent a considerable amount of time in hospitals. Even then, they were reluctant to talk about their experiences. There might have been an occasional outburst of disgust at the very mention of anything related to Japan, but no-one was encouraged to ask questions.

In my later years I came to know a few former POWs, but on joining the staff of Newcastle Borough Council I had the privilege of working with and befriending two particular colleagues who had served in the Far East during World War II. Today, thanks to the media, anyone can be classed as 'a hero', but these two men were heroes in the true sense of the term, and the fact that they survived the war is nothing short of a miracle. It was only in later life that I learned a little of their experiences although, even then, they were reluctant to talk about them. One had been in Changi for the most part of the war in the most appalling conditions with poor food, where there were large numbers of cases of diarrhoea, cholera, and various fevers. He had witnessed the brutal treatment of fellow prisoners including the horrific murder by bayoneting of a group of Gurkhas. The medical officers at the camp had worked wonders with what little equipment and drugs they had, but those who eventually liberated the jail described the whole scene as 'completely unreal.'

Badge of Wingate's Chindits. *(Richard Durrant).*

The other colleague survived Dunkirk only to be posted to the Far East where he joined the famous Wingate's Chindits. Formed by Major General Orde Wingate, the Chindits were a guerrilla-type force specialising in long-range penetration warfare against the Japanese in the jungles of Burma. It was said that *'they marched in the jungle, lived in the jungle, and fought in the jungle'* beating the Japanese at their own time honoured tactics. But my friend said *'it was hell on earth'* for those involved, having to cover *'50 miles a day in dense jungle.' Sometimes they lived 'in their own dirt for weeks - there was no time to stop. Those who could not keep up just had to drop out and were never seen or heard of again.'*[4] Having been wounded, he spent a period in a Calcutta hospital where the patients were visited by forces' sweetheart Vera Lynn. She held his hand whilst singing a requested song and left her autograph which he naturally treasured. On his return to England, he spent two years in Netley Hospital, Southampton. For years after, his health was affected and at times he had to receive treatment at Birmingham's Tropical Diseases Unit.

Both colleagues never fully recovered from their experiences, suffering from ill-health including flash-backs and innumerable nightmares until they died. Only then for them was the war finally over. Other families found themselves in the same situation, never fully appreciating what suffering their loved ones had endured and for what purpose. As the eminent historian Sir Martin Gilbert wrote *'there was no single day on which the Second World War ended.'*[5]

But if there were problems for ex-servicemen in picking up the threads of family life on their return, so there were for evacuees, more so for those who were long-term. Plunged back into bomb damaged towns and cities, some missed the countryside and the freedom they had come to take for granted. Whereas some parents did make efforts to visit their evacuated children, there were those who had not seen their off-springs for the whole of the evacuation period. The sudden transition back to the parental home came as a considerable shock, coupled perhaps with a returning father who they scarcely recognised. Some children were unable to settle and returned to their 'foster-parents'. There are examples of evacuees not returning and being adopted in North Staffordshire. In Silverdale, three evacuated sisters and a brother returned to London but a few days later, the 'foster-parents' returned to their home in Church Street to find one of the girls sitting on the doorstep! She pleaded to stay but it was decided that it was in the child's best interest that she should be returned to her parental home.[6]

Those born after this period might have gained the impression that life returned to normal within a few days of the Japanese surrender. This could not be further from the truth. The country subsequently faced years of austerity. Inevitably the nation had to concentrate on returning its economy and industry to peacetime production. Thousands of homes required repair or replacing resulting in a housing shortage. On the domestic front there was a hard slog with rationing

V. E. Day celebrations in Madeley Street, Silverdale. *(John Ankers).*

A postcard issued following World War II (*Author's collection*).

V. E. Day celebratory parade photographed in High Street, Silverdale with the Mayor, Councillor J. H. Ramsbotham taking the salute. *(Edwin Furnival).*

Church Street, Silverdale - taken in the 1960s by the late Jack Deakin prior to demolition.

continuing in some form until 1953. Also, during the long and bitter winter of 1947, when the level of snow was higher than our wellingtons, the country's fuel supplies almost ran out.

The Second World War was the worst of all conflicts, so far as casualties were concerned. Fifty-five million people lost their lives, including soldiers and civilians of every nation involved.

Notes

1) *Sentinel* 14th May 1945
2) *Staffordshire Advertiser* 18th August & 8th September 1945
3) See *The Fledglings* by same author. p91
4) Vincent James Reynolds. Letters to author 19th November 2003 & 15th December 2003.
5) Sir Martin Gilbert *The Day the War Ended* (Harper Collins) p407.
6) Ex information Mrs Christine Ward.

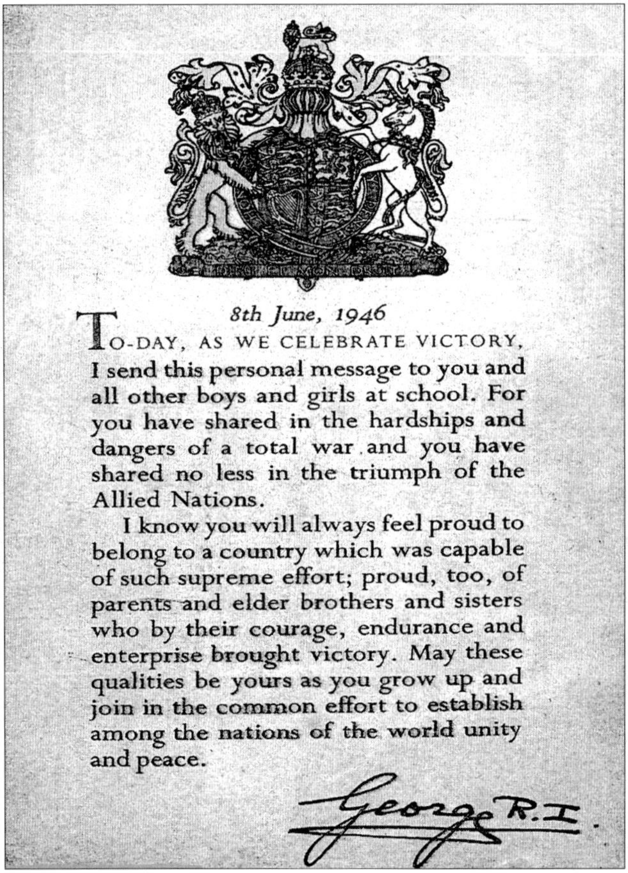

8th June, 1946

TO-DAY, AS WE CELEBRATE VICTORY, I send this personal message to you and all other boys and girls at school. For you have shared in the hardships and dangers of a total war and you have shared no less in the triumph of the Allied Nations.

I know you will always feel proud to belong to a country which was capable of such supreme effort; proud, too, of parents and elder brothers and sisters who by their courage, endurance and enterprise brought victory. May these qualities be yours as you grow up and join in the common effort to establish among the nations of the world unity and peace.

George R.I.

Scroll given to schoolchildren in recognition of their six years of childhood on the home front during World War II. *(Author's collection).*

Taken during mining of the last coal at Silverdale on the Ragman seam. *(Jack Dayson).*

My late father's colliery anvil, now at rest in a Silverdale garden. *(Author's collection).*

The Australian High Commissioner, the Hon. Neale Blewett, unveiling the Mining Memorial at Silverdale on 8th June 1996. *(Lynne Bebbington).*

Silverdale Colliery which sadly closed on 24th December 1998. *(The Sentinel).*

EPILOGUE

As I've often heard said, the war period was certainly no picnic for any of us. Susan Goodman states in her excellent book Children of War - *'five years of casualties, of official telegrams informing of death or capture of close relatives.... brought grief to so many families and sapped so much emotional energy.... For the survivors, nothing could ever be the same again.'*[1]

Attitudes and habits enforced by the war became engrained within us. Making the best of everything was continually drummed into us by parents and teachers alike. Rationing was the norm which resulted in a dislike of waste, particularly food. It was of little use informing parents that we didn't like an item which had been served up on a plate. As Mary Clews reminded me, we were likely to be told to *'eat it or leave it - there'll be nowt else!'*

Recycling everything possible became second nature. By constantly hearing *'it's wartime - you've got to get on with it!'* we learned to become adaptable, independent and thrifty but perhaps most important of all, grateful for what we had. The lack of toys was compensated for by the freedom we had to play outdoors for hours on end - and we came and went as we pleased, with the minimum of supervision. The old fashioned values - pulling together, hard work and patriotism helped to stand us in good stead for the years to come.

The Five Road Ends and most of the surrounding environs are no more, disappearing as part of the redevelopment of the central area of the village in the 1970s. As one Daleian quipped - *'what Hitler failed to destroy was achieved by planners!'* Common sense tells me that there is a great deal not to regret in the passing of the Five Road Ends, but one thing is certain, my friends from that period tend to agree that it was a good place to grow up.

Gone too is the mining industry. Part of the North Staffordshire coalfield, Silverdale Colliery instilled in its population a unique sense of pride and indomitable spirit that saw them through troubles and disasters. The closure of the colliery and the redevelopment of the central area of the village ripped the community asunder. That way of life has gone for ever.

Change is inevitable and no-one would wish for a return to the housing conditions of that time. Yet it was a happy, closely knit community which was broken up and dispersed. With perhaps a few exceptions, there is not the same neighbourliness today and our way of life is sadder without it.

Notes 1) Susan Goodman *Children of War* (John Murray) p320.